THE STORY OF THE BOOK

THE STORY OF THE BOOK

TERENCE COPLEY

This edition © Terence Copley 2005

First published in 1990 by the Bible Society.

ISBN 1 84427 131 5

Scripture Union, 207–209 Queensway, Bletchley, Milton Keynes, MK2 2EB, United Kingdom
Email: info@scriptureunion.org.uk
Website: www.scriptureunion.org.uk

Scripture Union Australia, Locked Bag 2, Central Coast Business Centre, NSW 2252, Australia
Website: www.scriptureunion.org.au

Scripture Union USA, PO Box 987, Valley Forge, PA 19482, USA
Website: www.scriptureunion.org

The right of Terence Copley to be identified as the author of this work has been asserted by him in accordance with the Copyright, Designs and Patents Act 1998.

Scripture quotations are from the Good News Bible, published by The Bible Societies/HarperCollins*Publishers* © 1966, 1971, 1976, 1992 American Bible Society.

British Library Cataloguing-in-Publication Data.
A catalogue record of this book is available from the British Library.

Consultancy by Sarah Lane
Printed and bound by CPD.
Cover design by Phil Grundy.

Scripture Union is an international Christian charity working with churches in more than 130 countries, providing resources to bring the good news of Jesus Christ to children, young people and families and to encourage them to develop spiritually through the Bible and prayer.

As well as our network of volunteers, staff and associates who run holidays, church-based events and school Christian groups, we produce a wide range of publications and support those who use our resources through training programmes.

For Claire, Nicky and Simon, with best love

Contents

Part Four: How did the Bible reach us?

Part Five: How was the Bible translated?

Part Six: How is the Bible read?

Preface

to the second edition

This book is the second edition of an original published by Bible Society in 1990. It was originally aimed at two audiences: pupils in secondary schools, especially those preparing for GCSE, and adults who for a variety of reasons wanted to know more about the Bible and its origins. Major changes have been made to the original text: omitting material that has gone out of date, adding material more relevant to a new century – including Bible translations that have appeared since the original book was written – and rewriting large parts of the text into today's English. The main audience for this book is no longer the GCSE student but the general reader, young or old, churched or unchurched, over the whole spectrum from sheer curiosity about the Bible or the Christian faith to strong Christian commitment. Questions are added for individual readers to think about, or for people using the book in a group discussion. Secondary school students can still access the book using the index and contents list for their project or research work.

In the first edition I wrote that I had tried 'to make no assumptions about the background of readers. They may or may not be Christian. They may or may not know Bible stories, or have some background knowledge of the Bible. I hope they will find some basic questions answered about this Book of Books – as it is for the Christian faith.' That intention remains unchanged. The Bible is also a 'heritage text' for Britain, a text that – as part of a living religion, Christianity – has shaped much of the culture of this country: education, the legal system, the arts, the English language etc. As such, the Bible is a heritage text for all British people whether they are British Muslims, British Hindus or British humanists. But for Christians the Bible is a sacred or special text – much more than heritage or culture. For them it is a living text that can shape and change lives.

The tired half-joke about the Bible, that it is the 'best-selling, least-read' book is still going the rounds. But is it really true? We shall visit recent research into young people's attitudes towards the Bible, both in church groups and in Religious Education classes in school.

The Story of the Book is written for cover-to-cover reading, or to be dipped in and out of or used for reference, so occasionally an important fact might be mentioned in more than one chapter, just in case the reader is not journeying through the full book.

The Bible quotations in the book are from the Good News Bible (abbreviated to GNB). It will help to have a copy of the Bible to hand while reading, but it doesn't have to be a GNB.

The questions are intended to help you dig deeper into the issues brought up by each chapter. Of course, you do not have to do them! They are there as a guide for further study and to provoke discussion for those reading this book as part of a group.

Terence Copley
School of Education and Lifelong Learning,
University of Exeter,
Spring 2005

Part One

How did the Bible come together into one book?

1 Who decided what went in?

A glance at the contents page of any Bible will immediately show that although the various documents and books have been gathered into one book, there are 66 separate books within the one. Some of these 'books' are very short, like the Third Letter from John. Fitting 66 different books into one is why the Bible is sometimes compared to a small library. It holds different types of books: Torah, sometimes called religious law, history, poetry, dreams and visions, letters, and a special type of book called Gospels, literally translated 'good news'. The Gospels tell of the life of Jesus, but they are not, as some people imagine, biographies of Jesus in the modern sense of biography.

It seems clear from reading them that none of these books was written with the intention of being put into a collection of 66. So how did they get there? Who decided what went in?

Think for a minute about Christianity in its early years. It was a new religion, not highly organised, mainly unknown, with growing numbers of enthusiastic believers eager to share their faith with others. Jesus did not write a book. He never told his disciples in any detail how to run and organise Christian groups after him, so in the early days Christians had to learn as they went along. It was very much trial and error. There wasn't a clear set of instructions like people expect now when they sit exams or use model-making kits or cookery books. Nothing was laid down in writing. There were no rules about how to be a Christian and how to organise the Christian community. There were no priests, vicars, ministers or pastors as we know them today in the sense of a full-time professional group of leaders for churches. There were no church buildings. Christians worshipped in one another's homes. There was no Christmas for the first 300 years of Christianity. Instead, Easter was kept as the one major festival. Some Christians who were Jewish weren't even sure whether they were part of a new separate religion or a new branch of the Jewish faith. They still worshipped as Jews on *Shabbat* (Sabbath – a Saturday) and as Christians on Sunday. Christians had to decide issues as they went along and tackle problems as they cropped up.

Of course, they weren't alone. Jesus had promised his followers that God would send them the Holy Spirit, so they believed that in a very real sense Jesus was there to guide them. Those who had spent time with Jesus during his life on earth were also able to provide leadership at first: Jesus' brother James, the remaining 11 disciples, especially Peter, and some newcomers with strong leadership qualities, like Paul. These people gave guidance, sometimes contradictory, about what being a Christian meant. As the faith spread the leaders couldn't always travel round to see the different groups that were growing so rapidly, so they had to resort to writing letters to keep in touch, to deal with Christian questions and give advice. These letters were read out when the groups met together for worship, often very early on the first day of the working week, which in those days was Sunday. Sunday was special to Christians because of Jesus' resurrection. We can picture them in the early days, meeting in one another's homes before dawn, to celebrate and remember Jesus' death and resurrection together, praying, and perhaps hearing one of the letters read out from Paul or some other leader before quietly slipping away to the day's work.

Those Christians who were originally Jews (at first they were clearly the majority) already had a Bible. This was the Hebrew Bible, the Bible of Jesus. Many would have read a Greek translation of the Old Testament, which had been made almost two hundred years previously in the Egyptian city of Alexandria. Legend has it that it took 72 scholars to do the job. That is why it is called the Septuagint and is often referred to by the Roman number LXX, which means 70. This Bible also included a number of mostly historical and wisdom books which, as far as we know, did not exist in Hebrew. It was widely used in Christian churches (both the Greek and Hebrew versions) and later became known to Christians as the Old Testament. They would have read this and perhaps sung psalms from it. Certainly they believed it pointed to Jesus and that he had made it come true for them in an unexpected way. They believed he was the Messiah to whom it looked forward and that he was the climax of all its promises. So, although they used this Hebrew Bible, they began to use it and interpret it in a distinctively Christian way.

As time passed, the disciples and witnesses to the things Jesus said and did began to die or were killed horrifically, as happened to Peter. According to tradition he was crucified upside down during Emperor Nero's attack on the church in Rome. The word 'martyr' literally means 'witness'. Paul, as a Roman citizen, had the 'privilege' of being beheaded, which was quicker than crucifixion, even if the axe was blunt. Although Nero's attack on Christianity was a local one, limited to the Rome area and not the whole of the Roman empire, he caused the deaths of Peter and Paul, so the young church suddenly lost two of its leading figures. Despite this, the number of Christians continued to increase dramatically.

Who was then to tell newly baptised Christians about the faith and the details about Jesus? Christian groups began to collect material. Some wrote down what they had seen or gathered from others. So Gospels came into being, to tell the good news about Jesus. Christians also kept the letters. You didn't throw away a letter that was written by a well-known leader such as Paul, even if some of the issues it was written about had changed. Once these leaders died their letters were more precious.

So if we think about the second century AD we have to picture a rapidly growing Christian community, already scattered throughout the Roman empire, not organised as one single group, still having different leaders, some of whom claimed to follow on from the disciples. This community had various letters and Gospels, perhaps hundreds or thousands of documents altogether, but not collected in one place, or centrally listed for information. But that wasn't all. These first Christian groups – they can be called churches as long as we remember they didn't have church buildings – began to be troubled by the spreading of other, different documents. Some of these were fake gospels, perhaps created by opponents of Christianity in an effort to discredit it. They contained all sorts of unbelievable or even objectionable stories about Jesus, such as how he killed his schoolteacher. Other dubious gospels were no doubt by pious Christians who let their imaginations run away with them and fantasised all sorts of wild stories, often about Jesus' childhood or the missing years in his life, between 13 and 30, about which no real evidence survives. Where was Jesus during those years? Who was he with? Little wonder that some people gave him a wife and children, as one spurious gospel did. Perhaps it is not difficult to see how some people believed all this, when occasionally – still on no evidence – one of these stories is revived in the popular press or in a cinema film.

The result for the ordinary Christian was confusing. What were you to believe? How could you tell true from false? Which were the best books and letters to use? It was these problems that led some Christian leaders to issue lists, sometimes called canons, of approved books. The word canon came from a Greek word, *kanna*, meaning a reed or cane. It came to mean rule or ruler, something straight by which to judge if a line was straight. These canons of books were intended to let you check that the document you were going to read or listen to was approved, straight, OK. Now and again, because the Christians were not one tightly organised group, different lists emerged from different leaders, in different Christian centres.

The first surviving list came from a controversial man called Marcion, around the year AD 144. He had a strong dislike for the Jewish faith and for Jewish Christianity, so his list was a drastic pruning of the Bible we know. He omitted the whole of the Old Testament, selected Luke's Gospel only (and even then edited his own version of it), and included selected letters of Paul – Galatians, Corinthians (both letters), Romans, Thessalonians (both letters), Colossians, Philippians, and Philemon. He also included a mysterious letter, 'Laodiceans', possibly the one we know as Ephesians. Marcion liked Paul because Paul had become the leader of non-Jewish Christianity. Another list, now called the Muratorian Canon, dates from about the year AD 200. It includes in the New Testament the book of Wisdom, now available in the Old Testament Apocrypha (see page 24), and a book known as the Apocalypse of Peter, though the list notes doubts that this book was written by the disciple Peter. It missed out Hebrews, James, the letters of Peter, and the letter now known as 3 John. The Third Letter from John was also missed out by a prominent Christian of those times called Irenaeus. He let 1 Peter in but cut 2 Peter out. Other lists noted undisputed books, that everyone agreed were 'in', disputed books, and rejected books. The books we call the letter of James, Jude, Hebrews, 2 Peter, 2 and 3 John, and Revelation often fell into the disputed books lists. This was partly because there were disputes about whether they were written by the person whose name appeared as author.

This custom of listing recommended books, and the different lists, continued into the next century, the 300s. Lists varied from area to area, presumably because some Christian groups had some books not known to others and because they did not know about books possessed by other groups. Eventually one of the leaders, Bishop Athanasius, in an Easter letter to his Christian communities in AD 376, produced the list that became what we call the New Testament. An important Christian conference in Rome approved this list in AD 382 and another important conference in the north African city of Carthage in AD 397 approved it. So it became the superior list and gradually took over from rival lists. Some books failed to get into Athanasius' list. One, the book of Revelation, only just got in. So it was a bit like a top ten, or rather a top 27. What helped a book to get on the list was if it was generally accepted to have been by an apostle. The first Christians believed that a book by an apostle was a sort of guarantee: you could rely on it.

So in a way, the Bible as we know it 'grew'. No single person or group decided finally what went in, but the different lists emerged and eventually one was accepted over the others. Although the first Christians had their documents and books – the earliest is reckoned to be 1 Thessalonians, dated around AD 50 and the latest is estimated to be after AD 100 – they did not have a Bible, in the sense of the completed collection of approved books we call the Bible, until around AD 400.

To investigate further

1 Read Matthew 27:3–10 and Acts 1:18–20. What do these accounts agree on? What do they disagree on? Can you suggest reasons for the differences?

2 Read Acts 15 and Galatians 2:1–14. What do these passages show about conflict in the first Christian groups?

3 Read 1 Corinthians 11:17–34:
a) What was going wrong when Corinthian Christians met for communion?
b) How did Paul try to solve this in the advice he gave?
c) Which part of this passage does more than just settle matters that were issues at the time of writing, and is seen as so important that it is used regularly in Christian worship today?

Thought-prompters

1 Why do you think the letters of a Christian leader were viewed by Christians as more precious if, as in the case of Paul, the leader had been executed?

2 Why do you think that Marcion's list didn't catch on among the majority of Christians?

3 Why do you think most of the lists put the Gospels first, even though many of the New Testament letters were written before the Gospels?

4 Read 2 Peter 3:15–17. Remember that this was a 'disputed' book, and is thought to be one of the later books to be written in the New Testament.

a) What does it show has already happened to Paul's letters?

b) What does it show about the growing number of Christian writings?

c) What evidence does this passage contain to suggest that this letter might well be one of the later ones?

2 What was left out of the Bible?

With a selection process like that described in section 1, there were bound to be near misses. Fortunately some of the books that were left out survived in whole or in part and can be read now. But precisely because they were left out of the official lists of approved books, they are by no means as easy as Bibles to obtain. Here are some of them:

- I Clement (AD 96), a genuine letter from Clement, bishop of Rome to Corinthian Christians
- Seven letters by Ignatius, an early Christian leader, who died in about AD 107
- The letter of Polycarp
- The letter of Barnabas, said to be the friend of Paul
- The Didache (pronounced di–da–key), which means 'teaching' – an anonymous book
- The Gospel of Thomas, with alleged secret sayings of Jesus (see page 18). This turned up in 1945 in a sealed jar at the base of a cliff in Egypt. It is a teaching gospel, with no details about Jesus' life. It contains 150 alleged sayings of Jesus, roughly half of which appear in the New Testament's four gospels.
- The Gospel of the Egyptians, which reports an alleged conversation between Jesus and Salome, in legend the girl whose dancing half hypnotised Prince Herod and led to the beheading of John the Baptist (see Mark 6:14–29)
- The Gospel of the Hebrews, containing the story of Jesus' resurrection appearance to his brother James, who had sworn a religious oath not to eat until he had seen him – the first hunger strike!
- The Gospel of Peter, containing the strange idea that Jesus felt no pain at his crucifixion

- The Gospel of Mary (Magdalene, not Jesus' mother)
- There were also various Acts, written to copy the idea of Luke's second book, the Acts of the Apostles. So, for instance, there was an Acts of Paul and Thecla.

There were different reasons for books not appearing on a list. Some were thought to be doubtful or fake. Others were thought to be unsuitable because they weren't helpful enough for the spiritual life to be suited to public reading, but could be recommended for private reading.

At the same time, Jewish scholars had been trying to establish a canon of writings for what Christians now call the Old Testament. They kept all the writings of the Septuagint (see page 12) which had been originally been written in Hebrew. This is called the Masoretic text. They cut out the Greek writings which had no Hebrew original. These are called the Apocrypha. The word originally meant 'hidden', perhaps in the sense of having a meaning hidden from all but the wise. This appears between the testaments in some Bibles. Some Christians prefer to call this collection the Deuterocanonicals (meaning 'second canon'—see page 24). Others were thought to be too distant in time from Jesus and the disciples to be included in the lists.

In some cases a book only just scraped in. In the Hebrew Bible one such book is the Song of Songs. The debate about this focused on whether it was deeply symbolic of the relationship between God and Israel and so worthy of inclusion, or whether it was simply an erotic love song and as such unsuitable. With the New Testament book of Revelation, arguments were about how far it was apostolic, that is, written by a disciple. It was certainly written by someone called John, but the ideas and the style of writing make it seem to most scholars quite unlikely that it was the disciple John. Revelation's John, sometimes called the Divine, an old-fashioned name for a theologian or religious thinker, was in exile at the time on the Greek island of Patmos. He introduces himself to the reader in Revelation 1:9–11. In a series of apparently weird visions that would make an 18-Certificate horror film look tame, he sees a picture of terror and the downfall of the Roman empire because of its evil doings. Monsters, dragons, war, famine, heat, drought, blood, infernos, and magic numbers are all part of the cast and backcloth of these visions. The time of disaster so vividly described in the book is followed by a time of God's reign, a reign of happiness and peace described in the last two chapters. These have become best known today for their use in funeral services as words of comfort. It is perhaps fitting that the collection of 66 books that began with stories about creation (Genesis 1 and 2) should end with a vision of a new creation (Revelation 21 and 22).

To investigate further

See if you can get a copy of some of the excluded books and have a look at several. Libraries may have them in the two-volume edition called *New Testament Apocrypha* edited by W Schneemelcher, published by Westminster John Knox Press in 2003, or in The *Apocryphal New Testament* edited by J K Elliott (Clarendon Press 1993). The Gospel of Thomas exists in several paperback editions including a recent one edited by Stevan Davies, published in 2003 by Darton, Longman and Todd Ltd. If you can obtain any of them and read a few pages, think about:

a) points where they seem to use the recognised four Gospels, if you know them well enough;

b) whether they have a ring of truth or ring of falsehood about them;

c) what you think their original appeal may have been.

Thought-prompters

1 Why do you think the book of Revelation only just got in to the New Testament? One answer is suggested above. Read Revelation 6 for clues to a second answer. How Christian do you think these chapters are in their ideas?

2 Read 2 John. It's nice and short! Why do you think this book was included? There are clues above, as well as in the letter itself.

3 Jesus said: The Kingdom of the Father is like a woman who was carrying a jar full of grain. As she walked along a handle of her jar broke off [jars were multi-handled] and grain trickled out, but she didn't notice. When she arrived in her house, she put the jar down and found it empty. (Gospel of Thomas, Saying 97). What do you think this parable might mean? Could it be a genuine saying of Jesus? Why? Why not?

3 Where did all the books come from in the first place?

In a way, the only answer to this is more than 66 places. Although the one book that we call the Bible contains 66 books, they contain material from different sources, written at different times, so there is no easy answer to the question of where the books came from. It is easier to answer for some books than for others.

Take Luke and Acts, for example. Luke actually wrote what we would call a preface to both books to explain what he was trying to do. Interestingly, he reveals that there were a large number of writings before him (Luke 1.1) and then announces his intention to provide an orderly and reliable account for his sponsor Theophilus. So the easy answer to where Luke's Gospel came from is that Luke wrote it. As far as it goes, that's true. But where did he get his information? Luke himself was not a disciple and there is no suggestion that he personally met Jesus at all. One old tradition suggested that he was a painter. That conjures up an impression of Luke the artist wandering around Galilee, painting and talking to people about Jesus, and from that collecting the information for his Gospel. Appealing as that might be, it isn't backed by hard evidence. So it is no more than a guess. Another tradition, that Luke was a doctor, actually disagrees with it. More importantly, Luke's Gospel has a lot of overlap with the Gospel of Mark (at times almost word for word) and with parts of the Gospel of Matthew. That must mean one or more of them used one or more of the others as a source, or else they had a common source no longer surviving as a separate book. We shall look at this intriguing idea elsewhere. It's enough here to say that this view of Luke's Gospel, which implies he rather painstakingly used or adapted material from different sources, fits in entirely with what he says in the preface.

Behind all the Gospels (including Luke) come the sayings of Jesus, and teaching by him and about him. These were passed on by his friends and followers to the next generation of Christians. Perhaps they were remembered because of catchy sayings or phrases. Although it was probably at least thirty years between Jesus' resurrection and the first of our surviving Gospels, Mark, we must not assume that Jesus' words were forgotten or that incidents in his life would necessarily be distorted or mis-remembered. Not only is there evidence that memory was better trained then (we shall examine this later), but it is commonplace now for people of forty and older to remember perfectly significant events that took place thirty or more years before. It is only when they try to remember last week that elderly people get stuck! They can remember events in their childhood very clearly.

Much of the material that forms the Bible had its beginning in oral telling and in memory. In the Old Testament, the narratives about the patriarchs, or fathers, of Israel – Abraham, Isaac, Jacob – must have been in circulation for centuries before they were written down in the 'book of Beginnings' (Genesis). It is easy to imagine these stories being told around a campfire when we read Genesis 18:1–15, where Abraham and Sarah tangle with the messengers of God. The Hebrew tribes must have told and retold these narratives during their desert wanderings. Moreover, scholars confirm that some of the customs described in these narratives are genuine survivals from the age in which the stories began. They have other ancient literature as supporting evidence, and archaeology can sometimes provide evidence of customs as well.

Letters, of course, originate with their writer, so the source of the letters of the New Testament is easy – they started life as written documents, though the name of the writer is not always known. Some parts of the Old Testament started in written form. There is evidence that King David employed a court secretary who kept records (2 Samuel 20:25) and some of the material that appears in 2 Samuel could have come from this source. An old tradition says that the lyrics to the hymn book of the Old Testament, the book of Psalms, were written by David. Many people think that, although the psalms contain material from David himself, the evidence of the language and ideas suggests strongly that they come from various sources at various times in Israel's history.

The chief part of the Hebrew Bible (= Christian Old Testament, see page 22), the Torah (sometimes called Law), which forms the first five books, comes from varied sources which could be described as tribal memories, history, law, genealogy (a sort of family tree), and ancient Hebrew poetry.

The books grouped together as Prophets, a word better understood as spokespeople for God than as tellers of the future, are probably derived from their teachings, as remembered by their students or disciples. This may be especially so where their words are introduced by the phrase 'the Lord says', which may refer to a particularly deep or direct inspiration they felt they had received, rather than a personal opinion. This phrase 'the Lord says' is dotted through various books of the Prophets. These include the books of Amos, Hosea, and Isaiah, and disciples of these men may have particularly valued those sayings. Jeremiah had his own secretary, Baruch, who took notes by dictation, though writing on a scroll and not a note pad (Jeremiah 36). The book of Ezekiel keeps talking about 'I' and could have been written or dictated by the man himself. In the collection of between-the-Testaments books called the Apocrypha, the book of Ecclesiasticus ('Sirach' in some Bibles) contains a detailed foreword. Here the translator, the grandson of the author Joshua or Jesus (not *the* Jesus) explains why he translated the book and the difficulty he had in places translating the Hebrew into Greek. He remarks frankly: The translations [of various religious books] differ quite a bit from the original.

That famous writer 'Anon' has a place in the Bible. The book of Malachi simply means 'my messenger', but the name of 'my messenger' is not revealed. The letter 'to the Hebrews' doesn't have a 'from'. There are other books of unknown authorship.

So it is impossible to provide a simple answer to the question of where the books of the Bible came from in the first place. What they have in common, however, is that they were produced by a person or group within the faith community, Jewish or Christian, to help that community understand its calling, duty, or job in the light of its past experience. None of it was intended as textbook history in the sense of history for the sake of history. Rather, we must understand that its first purpose was to make Jews better Jews (the Hebrew Bible/Christian Old Testament) and Christians better Christians (the New Testament); or, as the writers might have seen it, to make their readers more aware of God's actions and plans.

To investigate further

1 Ask any elderly person about their early adult memories. How accurate would you say their memories are? What helped you decide this? If you are looking at this issue in a group, compare your findings with others. What is there to test accuracy against?

2 Flick through the book of Isaiah and do a rough estimate of the frequency or total of 'the Lord says' phrases. What do you think that shows about the importance of the phrase?

Thought-prompters

1 If children remembered accurately the stories told by their grandparents about when they were young adults, and in due course told them to their own grandchildren, roughly how many years would be covered between the first events (the grandparents' young adulthood) and the great-great-grandchildren hearing the stories?

2 Why do you think that in the earliest days of Christianity people were not interested in Jesus' childhood?

3 What evidence does the Bible contain that might imply that not all Christians regard the details of Jesus' birth as important? Read the openings of all four Gospels.

4 Read the story of Jacob's dealings with Laban (Genesis 28–31), and consider:

a) Are there any details that you think have a 'ring of truth' about them and were particularly remembered in the passing down of the story? List them and then compare your list with those of others in the group.

b) Some Christians prefer to name their church buildings after Bible names rather than saints' names. Why do you think some of these buildings have been called Bethel?

c) What ancient customs are referred to in this narrative? (Clues: marriages, mandrakes, payment for work.)

d) What is the meaning of the word 'nomad'? How do we know that this narrative comes from the nomadic times of the Hebrews and not from the settled times in Canaan/Israel?

5 What sorts of letters do you or members of your family keep? What get thrown away? Why? Have any survived in your family for a long time, eg wartime letters from members of the family who were away in the armed forces, or who were prisoners of war? What comparisons might be made between such letters and those included in the Bible?

4 Why two testaments, and is the old one the same as the Jewish Bible?

The word 'testament', if it means anything at all nowadays, conjures up the phrase 'last will and testament'. There is a connection, because in the Bible the word testament means solemn agreement. This is like a will, which expresses someone's solemn intentions for what will happen to their possessions after their death. In a will, the person whose will it is disposes of their property as they see fit. Testament is the same as another old word, covenant. The Jews of the Old Testament saw themselves as being in a special relationship with God; he would be their God, if they would obey him. That was the agreement or testament. It was God's 'will', as God saw fit. There was a covenant or testament with Noah (Genesis 9:8–17), with Abraham (Genesis 17:1–8) and supremely with Moses (Exodus 24). The spokespeople the Jews called prophets persistently called them to keep their side of the deal, to obey God as king. When things went wrong in national life they viewed it as a sign of the nation's failure to live up to the testament, just as some Christians do now. Jeremiah and Ezekiel called the Jews to a new testament, a covenant agreement, a covenant which would be kept in the heart, when past failures would be forgiven (Jeremiah 31:31–34). Perhaps Jesus referred to this at his last meal with his friends, when he talked about the wine being the blood that seals the new covenant that would be brought about by his death (Mark 14:23–25). Perhaps he meant that the new testament time is now. Christians saw the death and resurrection of Jesus as the sign of God's new agreement. So in time their special collection of 27 books became known as the New Testament, and the 39 they inherited from their parent faith, Judaism, became known as the Old Testament, the testament or agreement that had, so to speak, come true and been completed in the New.

Not surprisingly, Jews would not want to refer to these first 39 books, their Bible, as the Old Testament, because to them 'old' implies out of date or incomplete. They would say that the 39 books are neither out of date, nor incomplete. Their view might be that the Messiah, the promised leader from God, has still to come. To them, these books are *Tanakh*, an abbreviation like TNK for Torah (Law), *Nebi'im* (Prophets), and *Kethubim* (Writings). Just as the Gospels are at the heart of the New Testament to Christians, so the Torah is to Jews in the *Tanakh*. In fact for Jews, the 39 books are 24. They count the Torah as five and the Nebi'im (Prophets) as eight. In the *Tanakh* (Jewish Bible) the books of Joshua, Judges, Samuel, and Kings are counted as the four former prophets and Isaiah, Jeremiah, and Ezekiel as three later prophets. The *Tanakh* views the rest of the prophets, which are much shorter in length, as one book. There are only 12 of them and they would fit conveniently upon one scroll. The *Kethubim* (Writings) include Psalms, Job and Proverbs and the five books associated with the Jewish festivals (Song of Songs, Ruth, Lamentations, Ecclesiastes and Esther). The books of Daniel, Ezra-Nehemiah, and Chronicles are are presented as three books. The Jewish 24 books derive from scroll length, but the content of the *Tanakh*'s 24 books and the Old Testament's 39 books is exactly the same. To Christians, the two testaments tell the story of the before time and the after time, God's dealing with the Jews before Jesus, and God's dealings with the Jews and eventually non-Jews through Jesus. They see one as naturally leading to the other.

To investigate further

Use a Bible dictionary or concordance and look up the word covenant. It will tell you the basic meaning and list where the word is used in the Bible. Look up these passages and note what covenants are referred to. Also note any ancient customs connected with covenants (clue: blood).

Thought-prompter

What are the similarities between the way a group of friends and relatives might view a person's last will and testament and the way Jews and Christians view their Scriptures? What are the main differences?

5 What do we miss between the testaments?

In many Bibles nothing comes between the testaments except one or two sheets of blank paper or map pages. But between the completion of the last book in what was to become the Old Testament and the writing of the first letter in what was to become the New, Judaism did not lack leaders or writers. In this between-the-testaments period (we can't date it exactly, but many people think it stretched from about 200 BC to about AD 40–50) the Jews suffered considerable persecution. Their country was invaded and occupied first by the Greeks and then by the Romans. They struggled to achieve independence. Rumours abounded about saviours, messiahs, and leaders who would get them out of all this mess and bring in God's kingdom – a time of justice, peace, and freedom. Out of these troubled and unsettled times came a mixed bag of books, some of which were gathered into what is now called the Apocrypha by some, or the Deuterocanonical books (meaning a second-best list or canon) by others. Although some Christians have viewed them as just as important as the Old Testament, many have regarded them as second rate from a religious point of view, ie not as important as the Old and New Testaments. These books came to form part of the Septuagint, the Greek version of the Old Testament used by Jews outside Israel and by non-Jewish 'God-fearers'. In time, Christians who had no Jewish background and therefore couldn't read the Old Testament in Hebrew used it.

Fifteen books form the Apocrypha. Two books, 1 and 2 Maccabees, are different accounts of the turmoil caused by the Jewish revolt which started in 168 BC against the emperor Antiochus. The first covers the history of the period 175–134 BC. We should note that this is religious history. The writer sees God clearly at work in the events that are being described. There are other books of what the Jews called 'wisdom', wise and practical advice based on religious beliefs. One is called the Wisdom of Solomon and the other the Wisdom of Jesus son of Sirach (not *the* Jesus), otherwise known as the book of Ecclesiasticus, not to be confused with Ecclesiastes. The advice covers topics like duties to parents, giving to the poor, the dangers of big-headedness, how to choose good friends, and using your common sense. Also contained in this varied collection of books is perhaps the first detective story in the world, the story of Daniel and the image of the god called Bel. This statue was eating 400 litres of flour and 40 sheep and drinking 200 litres of wine a day. Despite the temple it was in being locked and sealed with the king's own seal last thing at night, the food and drink were still gone next morning. But detective Daniel had his suspicions and set a trap by... If you have a copy of the Apocrypha or Deuterocanonicals you can read the story for yourself.

The Apocrypha contains many heroic women. There is the Greek version of the story of Esther, which appears in Hebrew in the Old Testament. It is a very different version. Then there is the narrative of Judith in the book of Judith. She was a deeply religious widow who is said to have saved Israel at a time of appalling national crisis – the Jews would have enjoyed this narrative at a time when they were going through so many crises. There is Susanna, a Greek addition to the book of Daniel and, like the Bel story, short. This is a narrative of stunning beauty, of attempted seduction, and of incorruptibility even to the point of death. Encouragement to stand firm, to be incorruptible, not to compromise, was what the writer felt the Jews needed in those desperate years. So while Christians agree that the Apocrypha is not always the deepest religious material, it bridges the gap between the testaments and provides a fascinating insight and background to the world into which Jesus was born.

A different group of writings called the Pseudepigrapha (= 'false writings') date from between 200 BC and AD 200. Some of these are Jewish. Some are Jewish-Christian. Some of these are really retellings of Hebrew Bible/Old Testament narratives with legendary additions written from a faith perspective. Now they are of more interest to scholars researching the beliefs and background to the era in which Christianity emerged.

To investigate further

1 Choose and read one of the short books in the Apocrypha. Summarise the plot and list any religious ideas you can spot in the book.

Is it possible to tell from the book you have read why the Apocrypha was viewed as second best by some Christians? If you are working in a group compare your answer with those of others.

2 Read Sirach on behaviour at dinner parties (31:12 – 32:13). How much of his advice is practical? Do you think it is out of date? How far do you think his advice here is religious, or based on religious beliefs?

3 Read Sirach on caution in taking advice (37:7–15). Do you agree with him? Why? Why not? Is his advice here religious, or is it merely common sense?

4 Do an internet search on the Pseudepigrapha and see what you can find out about some of the individual books.

6 So where did the title 'Bible' come from?

In New Testament Greek the words *ta biblia* meant 'the books': any books. The singular word is *biblion*. It may come from the port of Byblos in Syria, which is known to have been an exporter of papyrus. This word *biblion* hasn't changed much in two thousand years, for in modern Greek it has become *biblio*. It comes through into English in words like bibliography. B*iblos* in old Greek originally meant the inner bark of the papyrus plant, from which, of course, books were made. Papyrus itself gave us our English word paper. So when the title 'Bible' was used, it carried the implication that this was the collection of books, the books you really ought to read, the right books. But as a title for the 66 books we call the Bible, it only really caught on in the fifth century AD. While the books of the Bible had been around for five centuries at least, the title 'Bible' hadn't. For a quarter of its history so far, Christianity did not talk about 'the Bible'.

7 Where did the titles of the separate books come from?

Nowadays a title seems straightforward. The author thinks it up, consults the publisher and when they agree, the publisher gives it a prominent position on the cover and on the first inside page, the 'title page'. The title of a book can make or break it. People often choose whether or not to buy it on the basis of the title and the cover and whether they seem interesting. The author's name also appears prominently. But some modern books are written under a pen name, so the name of the author we read on the cover is not necessarily the person's real name. Whether the author is known – pen name or not – can affect whether a book sells. A well-known author can always sell their next book. Or if the writer is not well known as an author but is well known in some other capacity, their book will find buyers. Pop stars, football players and politicians manage to publish their autobiographies relatively easily.

There are big differences and yet some surprising similarities with the world in which the Bible books were written. They didn't have title pages and they didn't have covers. Those would have wasted highly expensive paper. In any case a rolled scroll couldn't have a title page or cover. But ancient books would be respected if the author were famous. We might regard it as cheating to put someone's name on a book they had not written, but it wasn't thought dishonest in the ancient world. Similarly, we don't criticise a book that is supposedly by someone famous but in fact has been written for them, in their name, by a 'ghost writer', as they are called in the trade. A ghost writer is employed by a publisher to write the story of some well-known person for that person, because they are too busy or maybe not good at writing. The ghost writer tries to get inside the skin of the celebrity and say what he or she would have said had they been writing for themselves.

Ghost writing of books or newspaper articles is well known nowadays. Yet although the book never names or refers to the ghost writer – this would reduce its authority – there is no outcry about this being dishonest or cheating.

Sometimes people have felt the most honest course is to name the book after someone else. Remember, on a scroll there were no pages for a dedication. A writer might feel so indebted to someone else for the ideas contained in a book that it was only fair to credit this person as author. It was paying the highest compliment, saying in effect 'you have inspired me so much that without you this book could not have been written'. So we cannot assume that every Bible book is automatically by the person whose name is connected with it; few people now would say Moses was the author of the whole of the first five books, the Torah, especially since his death is described in some detail (Deuteronomy 34). His name would have established its authority in times past. Nor can we assume David wrote all the psalms or that Solomon, whose wisdom was legendary, wrote all the proverbs.

On the other hand we must not assume that the writer whose name is linked with a book is not the author. It is highly likely, for example, that the Gospels of Mark and Luke were written by those two people. They were not so well known in the first Christian community as to have their names borrowed to go on the front of books. Similarly, most of the letters linked with the name of Paul seem, from their Greek style and their ideas, to come from a single person and there seems no reason to doubt that this was Paul himself.

Of course, where authorship is not certain, opinions will differ. The Gospel of John is a case in point. There are those who urge that this was written by the apostle John, even though it may be dated to around the years AD 80–100 (though even that is not agreed by scholars). The apostle John could well have been alive then, it is argued, if he was about 20 when Jesus was crucified in about the year AD 30. People lived to just as great ages then as they do now, only many fewer made it to 100 years old than now. On the other hand, it is argued that the Gospel was written by someone close to the apostle, but after his time, and that it embodies much deep Christian reflection and thought on the part of this unknown writer. That could account for some quite big differences between this Gospel and the other three. For example, John has the over-turning of the money-changers' tables at the start of Jesus' preaching; the other Gospels have it in the last week of his life. Another view is that since John was a common name then as now, there may have been several Johns, which could have led to confusion about authorship. There is evidence that there were several Johns, even at Ephesus where the apostle is said to have lived after the resurrection.

What all this means is that work on the authorship of books of the Bible can be exciting detective work because nothing is absolutely certain. The important question with all the books in the end, however, is not who wrote them, but how reliable they are and what religious truth they contain.

Thought-prompters

1 Read the two accounts of Jesus in the Temple in Mark 11:15–19 and John 2:13–22 and consider:

a) Do you think we are looking at two separate incidents, or two different accounts of the same incident? Why?

b) Can you think of any reason why, if it is the same incident, it should appear in such different places in the two books?

c) Does it matter where it appears in the Gospel time scheme, or does it matter more whether it is reliably reported?

2 The speeches of Jesus in the Gospel of John are often very different from those reported in the other three. Read and compare John 14 and Mark 7 and consider:
a) Do these two passages seem different in style or in what is said?
b) Do you think that John might be recording private teaching given to the disciples and Mark recording public teaching given to the crowds? Mark refers to private teaching in verse 17.

3 Look at the old Hebrew titles of Psalms 139–145. In the GNB these are provided in the footnotes at the bottom of the page. One (Psalm 142) is said to have been written in a cave, when David was in hiding. Read the psalm and the account of the hiding (1 Samuel 22) and the evidence of David's musical ability (1 Samuel 16:14–23). Then consider whether you think it likely that this psalm comes from David himself. Why? Why not?

4 The book of Nehemiah is unusual in the Bible, because it appears to be autobiographical. Read from chapter 2 onwards until you reach a point where you feel you've picked up the flavour of the writing. Don't go further than the end of chapter 7 anyway. Then consider:
a) Does it seem reasonable to accept that Nehemiah is the author? Why? Why not?
b) How far do you think he is telling the story from his own point of view?
c) What sort of man do you think he was on the basis of what you have read? Kind? Cunning? Deeply religious? A good organiser? Brave? Try to think of reasons for your choice.

8 Why 'Holy' Bible?

The word holy originally had to do with things that were special, different, set apart, even taboo or untouchable. It came to mean worthy of great respect, because of a thing's religious value. Thus it was said that saints were holy, or that their bones were, or that matrimony (marriage) was holy. So the words Holy Bible began to appear on the covers of some editions. If these Bibles were printed in fine leather covers in red or black, with perhaps gold edges to the pages, it was a sign that the book was different, special, or set apart. In this way publishers and printers showed their desire to produce a book that looked worthy of its contents and would be treated with very great respect by Christian readers. Many publishers and printers were committed Christians who believed in the book they were producing and wanted their product to be worthy of God. It reflected their best efforts. Of course, fashions change and people have different priorities. Christians want the Bible to be accessible to everyone and some people would be more likely to look at a paperback or book with a popular cover than a very grand or solemn one. So Bibles are produced to suit. But for gift Bibles, some people felt strongly that the word 'Holy' should feature on the cover.

In some church services, such as a Roman Catholic Mass, the Gospel reading is referred to as the Holy Gospel. It is a sign of respect, part of the same respect that is expressed if the congregation stands for the reading. But the word holy puts some people off because it seems goody-goody or too good to be true, or gives the impression that because the Bible is holy you shouldn't ask questions about it, or read it like any other book. This is a misunderstanding caused by the problem of changing fashions, not of clothes, but of words. Sympathy now means feeling sorry for someone; it used to mean feeling the same as them. Trespasses in the old Lord's Prayer used to mean wrongdoings; it now means going on to someone else's property without permission. Holy didn't use to mean something too good to be questioned. It used to be a compliment, but its meaning has perhaps changed in everyday English. But where a Bible carries its own title, Good News Bible, for example, or New Jerusalem Bible, or Revised English Bible, the possible problem of putting off readers is removed.

To investigate further

1 Look up 'holy' in a good dictionary. Would you be pleased or insulted to be described as a holy person? Why?

2 Imagine you are commissioned by a leading publisher to design a cover for a new edition of the Bible. How would you go about it? Would you go for a picture or a symbol on the cover? Why? Which picture or symbol? Something fairly traditional or something you yourself designed? Why? What colours would you choose? What precise title would you put on the cover? Why? Would you use Holy Bible? Why? Why not?

Thought-prompter

Find as many different Bibles as you can and list the words and pictures or symbols they have used on the cover, along with the date when they were published. You'll find the date in one of the first inside pages. Can you detect any trends in the fashion of Bible covers?

9 What about the writings of famous Christians who lived after the Bible was completed?

There have been many spiritual writings that Christians find helpful and even inspiring. John Bunyan's *Pilgrim's Progress* has become a classic of English literature. The works of CS Lewis are read and watched on screen productions by millions. The sermons of Charles Haddon Spurgeon are regarded as masterpieces of public speaking. It is rumoured that Queen Victoria went in disguise to listen to them. The hymns of Charles Wesley, like 'Hark, the Herald Angels Sing', regularly inspire Christians throughout the world. But however well received they are, or ever will be, they will never be universally regarded as having the same authority as the sermons, parables and hymns contained in the Bible. For both the Old and New Testaments there came a time when the canon (list of books) was seen to be closed and could not be added to. In all religions, books that are viewed as Scripture cannot be added to or deleted from. One can argue about what the texts mean, but not whether they should be included.

With the Christian writings of the New Testament one of the main points for including a book was if it was thought to have been written by an apostle, ie a follower who had known or experienced Jesus personally. Some of the early church leaders like Polycarp, Ignatius, and Justin Martyr wrote many letters and books, but they weren't apostles, so however good their work might be it was never seriously considered for inclusion in the New Testament. Instead, their work became the first in a long line of memorable Christian writings that will never be regarded as Scripture. Opinion as to exactly how they should be regarded in comparison with the Bible differs amongst Christians. Some maintain there are Christian writings outside the Bible which show every sign of being just as inspired by God as those inside it. The books included in the Bible give us our fullest and closest account of the life of Jesus, the first Christians, and the relationship between God and the Jewish people. However, so this argument goes, their inclusion had more to do with their timing, rather than the special insights they contained. Other Christians would feel very wary of such a view and insist that however good other writings might be, they can only be 'inspiring' and not 'inspired' by God in the same way as the Bible. The writings of the Bible represent a special, unrepeatable act of revelation by God, who can be seen as working behind and through the process by which they came to be selected and placed into one final collection. That gives the Bible an authority not possessed by any other Christian book.

Certainly, non-biblical books will never be given the same high status as those in the Bible. However helpful they may be to individual Christians, they will not be read publicly at every church service, form the basis of the majority of sermons, or become the subject of countless home study groups. For every Christian there will always be something undeniably unique about the Bible. Unlike many modern films with their sequels, we should never expect a 'Bible Two'.

To investigate further

1 Find out about one of John Bunyan's books and its plot or story. Perhaps read an extract if you can obtain a copy. Compare it to any part of the Bible that you have read.

2 Carry out a small survey among Christians you know into what religious books (if any) they read as well as the Bible.

Thought-prompters

1 What famous Christians alive now might expect to be remembered and read in a hundred years' time?

2 We live in an age of TV, film, video, CD-ROM, DVD. Can you think of any Christian appearing on screen who may still be watched in the future? Why?

3 What sort of qualities do you think Christians admire in their heroines or heroes?

Part Two

Who wrote the Bible?

10 What sort of people were the authors?

With modern books we have very easy answers to this question because so often the publisher provides a paragraph or two about the author at the front or back of the book, often including a photograph. Indeed, we might feel that in some way we know the writer. Clearly, the Bible does not provide that sort of information. But before we start to feel sorry for the Bible, we ought to look more carefully at the books of our time. The cover page often tells us about the writer's educational background, family, and hobbies, but none of this may be very relevant or tell us much about the sort of person the writer is. We learn more by actually reading the book and 'meeting' the writer through the way in which the story is told, seeing the things the writer applauds or condemns, what they choose to emphasise in the personal lives of their heroes and heroines. It's not so different with the Bible. The main information about the writers has to be gathered from careful detective work on their book. We find clues in the words, the ideas, the style of writing, what they emphasise about God, and the other themes and ideas they choose to include in their book.

We know, for instance, that Mark is mentioned several times in New Testament books outside his Gospel. The house church at his mother's was probably well known to readers of Acts. Mark himself was a relatively minor figure in early Christian missionary work. His Gospel is written in a direct, waste-no-words style, which perhaps accounts for one tradition outside the Bible in which Mark is remembered by the nickname 'Short fingers'. Certainly he presents the narrative in an almost breathless way, and the phrase 'at once' frequently appears. Mark might even be the anonymous and perhaps bashful young man who escaped from the soldiers in the garden of Gethsemane by slipping out of the blanket he had thrown round himself. It is a most curious detail to record if Mark were not the man. Then, the biggest puzzle of all, Mark's Gospel leaves us with the mystery of a missing ending (see Mark 16:9).

Luke also is revealed in glimpses outside his Gospel. His style of Greek isn't breathless and rushed but careful and educated. He quotes the Greek version of the Old Testament, as the Good News Bible reveals in its appendix entitled 'Septuagint Readings'. It is known that Luke was a Gentile (non-Jew) and his Gospel records a number of incidents involving Jesus and women. Jews of that time would not have felt it proper for a religious teacher to have dealings with women, other than with his own relatives, and might not have recorded such incidents. Luke did. As a non-Jew he didn't share Jewish scruples on this issue. This sort of detective work helps to piece together a picture of the man behind this non-Jewish Gospel and, incidentally, its sequel, the Acts of the Apostles, which we tend not to connect with it because of the order of books in our New Testament. Compare Luke 1:1–4 with Acts 1:1 ff. It may be that Luke appears in Acts in person as part of the 'we' referred to in a number of passages, eg Acts 16:11–16. On the other hand, this could be his way of indicating that he is using a first-hand source here in his account. Ancient books didn't add footnotes or acknowledgements to show where they'd come from, but they did sometimes copy the extract word for word as a way of showing the reader that they were using another source. Certainly, in his introduction Luke stresses his concern for truth and history.

Another writer who tells the reader quite a bit about himself is the writer of the book in the Apocrypha known to us as 2 Maccabees. He set out to summarise a five-volume history by Jason of Cyrene and comments:

> *The number of details and the bulk of material can be overwhelming for anyone who wants to read an account of the events. But I have attempted to simplify it for all readers; those who read for sheer pleasure will find enjoyment and those who want to memorise the facts will not find it difficult. Writing such a summary is a difficult task, demanding hard work and sleepless nights ... The historian must master his subject, examine every detail, and then explain it carefully, but whoever is merely writing a summary should be permitted to give a brief account without going into a detailed discussion. So then, without any further comment, I will begin my story. It would be foolish to write such a long introduction that the story itself would have to be cut short.*

(2 Maccabees 2:24–26,30–32)

This writer adds a rather stylish conclusion to his book:

> *The city of Jerusalem remained in the possession of the Hebrew people from that time on, so I will end my story here. If it is well written and to the point, I am pleased; if it is poorly written and uninteresting, I have still done my best. We know it is unhealthy to drink wine or water alone, whereas wine mixed with water makes a delightfully tasty drink. So also a good story skilfully written gives pleasure to those who read it. With this I conclude.*

(2 Maccabees 15:37–39)

Perhaps the New Testament writer about whom most is known is Paul. Although he appears as a major figure in Luke's second book, Acts, we get a vivid picture of him from his own letters. In one he briefly tells part of his life story (Galatians 1:11 – 2:14). So Paul is easy to get to know.

With some of the other books, however, the authorship is almost impossible to trace. Where the book or letter is short, we can only guess about the sort of person who wrote it from the brief contents available to us. The letter to the Hebrews is one such anonymous Christian document. Indeed it isn't even clear any more what precise group 'the Hebrews' were or what area they lived in, so although Christians value this document because it contains, among other things, a great piece of writing about what faith means, its author remains unknown by name or personality. Similar cases exist in the Old Testament. Malachi in the book of that name is not the name of a person. It means in Hebrew 'my messenger', which looks like a deliberate attempt at anonymity by the writer, who instead wants to stress their attempt to speak God's message for that time.

Some books contain material gathered or written at different periods of time and only later put together, so that they properly have several authors and at least one editor as they grew into the single book we see in the Bible now. In the case of the Torah (the first five books of the Christian Bible and the most important part of the Hebrew Bible), it is widely held that various people have over a long period of time produced documents or passed on oral memories and traditions. These were compiled into five books at a later date. Some scholars think that there were four main sources for these books and they have labelled them J, E, P and D. These names are codes from the first letters of key Hebrew words they use or traditions they represent. The theory is that these traditions were finally mixed together into the five books we have now. It would be interesting to see the material the compilers left out, if they didn't use it all, but unless some dramatic discovery of genuine and missing texts occurs – and in rare cases like the Dead Sea Scrolls such discoveries are made – we shall never know the answer to that.

It is important to note that the people who wrote the books of the Bible were not professional writers in the modern sense. That doesn't just mean that they lacked the modern technology of word processors and the internet. Their lives were also different in that, unlike a best-selling novelist, they didn't earn a living by writing, or even a part-time income as many other modern writers do. They wrote out of conviction or belief, for a purpose, not for fame or money. Indeed, since many of the first Christians believed that the Parousia (the return or Second Coming of Jesus) would shortly occur it is most unlikely that they thought their writings would last for many years. If you think that the world as you know it is shortly going to end, you don't plan to write a book to last for two thousand years.

Some of the New Testament letters are practical documents, written for the needs of a particular Christian group. Although Christians may still find them helpful and inspiring it is important not to lose sight of their original purpose and audience. That books in the ancient world were very expensive and therefore precious was a result of the costs of hand copying and not the result of a fat fee for the author. In fact, there is no evidence that any of them was paid even one denarius, a working man's wage for a day. There were few copies, all handwritten, and some were read aloud in Christian groups, with the people who couldn't read listening. Despite what is wrongly assumed nowadays, a large proportion of people could read. Fewer could write well, though we have no way of assessing exactly how many could read or write. The more copies of a modern book are printed the cheaper the selling price is per copy. This could not apply in a pre-printing age.

To investigate further

Spend about fifteen minutes reading the letter of James carefully. Then decide:
a) whether you think the writer was Jewish or Gentile (non-Jewish) and why;
b) what evidence in the letter itself suggests that the writer was Christian?
c) whether you can find any clues as to the sort of person the writer was (refer to particular verses in the letter in your answer).

If you find the answers hard, reread these key verses: James 1:1,9–11; 2:1–13, 14–17,21.

Thought-prompters

1 How far is it helpful to know what sort of people wrote the books of the Bible? Does the human-interest angle we are so used to in the modern media help or hinder our appreciation of any book?

2 The famous Methodist minister and preacher, WE Sangster, wrote a book entitled *Why Jesus Never Wrote a Book*. Why do you think Jesus never wrote a book?

3 Reread the extracts from 2 Maccabees that appear above and answer:
a) What can we learn about the writer's aims from these passages?
b) How far would what this person wrote about his summary apply to a modern-day attempt to reduce five volumes to one?

4 Read the Galatians extract referred to above (Galatians 1:11 – 2:14). What sort of person does Paul appear to be from this passage?

11 Why did they write?

Read any book, even if it doesn't have a title, and you can work out its main theme or purpose. If you have a gardening book, a cookery book, and a car-repair book, all without covers and title pages, you would be most unlikely to mistake them and to put a spanner in the cooker, a carburettor in the cabbage patch, and a bedding plant in the fuel tank. Every book has a theme, and even if the basic subject is the same you can still tell whether you are looking at a car-repair guide for idiots, or for DIY people who spend each weekend lying under their car, or whether it is the professional text for garages. This is the case with the New Testament. There are four Gospels, but they are not the same. It isn't just that they don't have the same writer. Their subject or theme is different. If we were going to give them titles we could call them:

The Mystery and Power of Jesus by John Mark; *Jesus, the Giver of the New Religious Law* by Matthew; *Jesus, the Man for Others* by Luke; *The Cosmic Christ* by John.

The purpose of the writer was to present the good news of Jesus as he saw it, to say who Jesus was rather than to list what he did. In fact the fourth Gospel refers to the impossibility of listing all the things Jesus did:

> Now, there are many other things that Jesus did. If they were all written down one by one, I suppose that the whole world could not hold the books that would be written.

(John 21:25)

What the Gospel writers have done, therefore, is to select material to fit their theme.

Luke and Acts are both by Luke. His theme is really to trace the good news from the birth of the forerunner, John the Baptist, which is where the Gospel of Luke begins, to how the good news reached the centre of the civilised world, Rome, which is where Acts ends.

In some Bibles there is a brief introduction to each book, prepared by the modern publisher, which sets out the main themes so that the reader is prepared for them as they occur in the text. This is the case in the Good News Bible and in the New Jerusalem Bible, for instance.

Some of the themes of the Bible books were controversial in their time. The book of Jonah, for instance, tells of a religious spokesperson or prophet, Jonah, who tried to run away from God's command and had various adventures, including the well-known encounter with the large fish. But behind the story lie important religious ideas: that God would always forgive rather than punish and that God is the God of all nations, not just the Jews. The book of Ezra was harder on the non-Jews and enables us to see just how controversial the issue was at the time. So Jonah is the story of particular people at a particular time. But it is more than this. It carries a very clear religious message. Communicating that message is the intention of the book. In fact, it would be very difficult to find anything in the Bible that was 'just' a story. Whether we are dealing with story or history, the Bible writers are trying to tell their readers something of God's purposes and intentions for people. Every book has its theme or purpose. No Bible book is merely a story.

To investigate further

1 The letter to Philemon was written to ask a specific favour. What was it? (Read 8–22.)

2 Read the book of Jonah.

a) In what way does the incident of the plant sum up the whole book? The clue lies in the last two verses of chapter 4.

b) If you were given the job of choosing a modern title for the book, what would it be?

12 What languages did they use?

The Hebrew Bible/Christian Old Testament was written entirely in Hebrew except for a small amount which is in Aramaic (not to be confused with the language of the Qur'an, Arabic). Aramaic had become more widespread than Hebrew by the very end of the Old Testament period. It only appears in our Bibles in parts of Daniel and Ezra and a few minor phrases elsewhere, but it was widely spoken. The state of Israel revived Hebrew as a language and plenty of books are available for tourists and visitors who want to learn either a little or a lot. But this has happened largely since the Second World War. The earliest Hebrew script (way of writing) survives very little, mainly among the very small Samaritan community in Nablus, descended from those referred to in Jesus' parable of the good Samaritan and in a few other places in the Gospels. The Hebrew in which the Old Testament is written is known as Square Hebrew. You can see why.

בראשית ברא אלהים את השמים ואת הארץ: והארץ
היתה תהו ובהו וחשך על־פני תהום ורוח אלהים

The square script was borrowed from Aramaic. It is now unchangeable and in fact has not changed significantly in two thousand years. Strict rules set out in a Jewish book of religious teaching called the Talmud make big change impossible. Obviously, Hebrew is written with a different alphabet. It is also written from right to left. It originally had no vowels, and when it was widely spoken this didn't produce problems. When people ceased to speak it, problems multiplied. Vn n nglsh t cn b hrd wrk t rd wtht vwls! By the sixth century AD a group of Jewish scholars called the Masoretes invented a system of vowels so as to make pronunciation easier. Here is the sample from above, with their vowels added. The vowels were written round the sacred words of the text so as not to disturb or alter them. The passage from which this sample was taken is the beginning of the book of Genesis.

בְּרֵאשִׁית בָּרָא אֱלֹהִים אֵת הַשָּׁמַיִם וְאֵת הָאָרֶץ: וְהָאָרֶץ
הָיְתָה תֹהוּ וָבֹהוּ וְחֹשֶׁךְ עַל־פְּנֵי תְהוֹם וְרוּחַ אֱלֹהִים

The New Testament was written in Greek. This was the common language of the Roman empire when Christianity began. The Greek of the New Testament, however, is not what some books call Hellenistic or Attic Greek. Those both mean the Greek of Greece, classical Greek. The Greek of the New Testament is common Greek, everyday Greek, sometimes called *Koine* (pronounced coin-ee) Greek, the Greek of the market place.

Ἐν ἀρχῇ ἦν ὁ λόγος, καὶ ὁ λόγος ἦν πρὸς τὸν θεόν, καὶ θεὸς ἦν ὁ λόγος. οὗτος ἦν ἐν ἀρχῇ πρὸς τὸν θεόν. πάντα δι' αὐτοῦ ἐγένετο, καὶ χωρὶς αὐτοῦ ἐγένετο οὐδὲ ἕν. ὃ γέγονεν ἐν αὐτῷ ζωὴ ἦν, καὶ ἡ ζωὴ ἦν τὸ φῶς τῶν ἀνθρώπων· καὶ τὸ φῶς ἐν τῇ σκοτίᾳ φαίνει, καὶ ἡ σκοτία αὐτὸ οὐ κατέλαβεν.

Some of the letters here may be familiar to you from mathematics. Can you spot any? The same alphabet survives in modern Greek, though the grammar and language of modern Greek are more streamlined even than that of the New Testament. Despite the 2,000-year gap, however, it is still true that if you learn one form of Greek you can fairly quickly learn the other. Within the New Testament books the style of Greek varies, as you would expect from different writers. Luke's (one tradition has it that he was a doctor) is educated Greek, as is Paul's. The Greek of Revelation is so bad, however, that it looks like the French homework of someone who might be advised to choose another subject if they wanted to pass an examination. Whether the writer couldn't speak or write Greek well, or whether he deliberately used this 'barbaric' Greek, as some have called it, to voice feelings in a forceful way is a matter for debate.

Throughout its pages, the text of the New Testament invites detective work. Even in places where the Greek is good there are some rather odd expressions. This leads scholars to question whether there are Aramaic echoes under or behind the Greek of the New Testament, suggesting that sayings of Jesus might have been preserved in the Aramaic he spoke and only translated into Greek later, or perhaps Aramaic Gospels existed alongside or before the Greek ones. The problem is that we only have the Greek ones to work back from and so it all rests on clever analysis of phrases. Some English-language Bibles such as the Authorised Version have phrases like 'he answered and said'. These are unnecessary in English. A teacher would correct it in an essay and prefer either 'he answered' or 'he said' or even 'he said in the answer'. But Aramaic used that as a common expression and it has survived into Greek. To exaggerate the sort of detective work involved, look at this passage in English:

> It is necessary to me to write this passage. I have twenty years. And it is one hour less the quarter to the party of my anniversary. My friends will wish me a good birthday. But I will keep my name secret and use the name of a pen instead.

It ought not to be too difficult to see that we are reading English, but written by someone who doesn't speak it well or has another language background. Can you work out which? (It's French!) Unfortunately the New Testament evidence is nowhere near as certain as this.

There is also a Greek version of the Hebrew Bible/Christian Old Testament, produced by Jews who were scattered throughout the Greek and (later) the Roman empires. Legend said it was produced by six translators from each of the 12 Hebrew tribes, taking 72 days. They worked separately on an island away from everyone but their translation was found to be identical, thus showing they had faithfully transmitted God's revelation from the Hebrew Scriptures into Greek. From this legend comes the Greek name for the translation, the Septuagint, sometimes abbreviated as LXX, coming from the word for 70 in Latin. Well, that's the story! What is clear, however, is that this translation came from Alexandria in Egypt, that it was fairly literal in parts, sticking word for word to the Hebrew but written in fluent Greek in other parts, which is good evidence that more than one person produced it. The Septuagint included books that are part of the Apocrypha in some Christian Bibles. Luke and Paul seem to quote it in their writings rather than the Hebrew version. It may be quoted in other New Testament writings too. The Greek word for the Torah is the Pentateuch (penta- means five), and in some textbooks this word is used in preference to Torah. But the books are the same, the first five books of what to Christians is the Old Testament.

Thought-prompter

One of the hardest decisions translators have to make is whether to stick very closely to the original language, which makes for an accurate translation, but often leads to odd English. On the other hand if they rewrite it into fluent English, some of the original meaning might be lost. What do you think they should choose to do?

13 How long did it all take?

According to many attempts at dating, most of the events written about in the Bible span the years from about 1900 BC to around AD 80–90, but the period of writing is different. Many of the events from the early period of the Hebrew fathers, Abraham and his descendants, were perhaps not written down for hundreds of years after they happened. Their accurate recall relied on the often remarkable capacity of the ancient eastern memory. Similarly, some of the documents in the New Testament were probably written around or even after AD 80–90.

Some of the Old Testament books began life as memories passed on by word of mouth. They were then written in some early form, and were later copied or edited into the books we now have. So the process of writing one book (as we now have it) could be a long and complex one. An example of this might be the book of Isaiah, which is named after a great spokesperson or prophet who lived in Jerusalem in the second half of the eighth century BC. The book seems to be divisible into three parts. Chapters 1–39, as we know them, contain material relating to the time when the kingdom of Judah was under threat of invasion from its mighty and massive neighbour, Assyria. These chapters record the words and actions of the prophet at the time of these events. Chapters 40–55 refer to a time when the disaster had happened and the Jews were in exile in Babylon. This section contains the famous 'Servant of the Lord' passages that the first Christians believed had been fulfilled by Jesus. Chapters 55–66 seem to refer to a time when the Jews had been, or were about to be, restored once again to Jerusalem and this section of the book gives them advice for their new situation.

All this would have taken centuries to happen. One theory is that the first section relates to the historical Isaiah, 'First Isaiah' as the theory calls him, and that the second section relates to 'Second Isaiah', who was perhaps a follower of the first one's teaching, but whose real name is not known. The third section, in this theory, is viewed as composite, ie as having various authors, but united in their being part of an Isaiah 'school' or tradition that preserved the prophet's message and teaching. They might have been, in this view, updating the prophet's teaching to show how it applied to their own time. This is one theory. Certainly some prophets had students or disciples. And Isaiah gave his instructions: 'You, my disciples, are to guard and preserve the messages that God has given me' (Isaiah 8:16). They would repeat and eventually write down the teaching.

Of course, some people believe that the book of Isaiah was written wholly or substantially by one man – Isaiah – with varying possibilities of editing and compiling of his material later by his disciples. This, too, could have been a long and complex process. So whatever theory may be correct about how the present book of Isaiah came to be written, it illustrates how complicated the origin of some of the Bible books may be. They may have grown over a period of time after the lives of the main characters portrayed in the book itself.

Occasionally, the Bible gives clues about the source material used by its writers. For instance, throughout the books of Kings and Chronicles we read the expression 'Everything else such and such a king did is recorded in "The History of The Kings of Israel", or "The History of the Kings of Judah".' So these books appear to use other writings as source material, which in turn presumably were written during the lifetimes of many different kings.

It is often easier to put dates on the events a book describes than to date the book itself. So, for example, the death of Herod the Great, the Herod of the Bethlehem toddler massacre, took place in 4 BC. This is known from sources outside the Bible. This means that Jesus was born before 4 BC, the calculation of the year zero having been made in the wrong place (it is out of place by about five years). It's too difficult to move it now because the history books would have to be rewritten: the Battle of Hastings would be recalculated to 1071. Herod's death and Jesus' birth can be dated. But the actual writing of the Gospel that tells the Herod story, Matthew, is harder to date. The writer probably knew Mark's Gospel and so came after Mark, generally dated around AD 65. The reference to a report being spread 'to this very day' in Matthew 28:15 suggests it was a long time after Jesus. Some people deduce from Matthew 23:37–39 that the Gospel was written after Jerusalem and its Temple had been destroyed by the Romans in AD 70. Taking all this into account, if we date the Gospel at AD 75–85 we shouldn't be far wrong. However, there is no universal agreement amongst scholars about dating the Gospels. It's all a question of interpreting evidence – sometimes slender evidence – and it is impossible to be more accurate. With John's Gospel the task of dating is still harder. It has been generally regarded for many years as a late Gospel, perhaps as late as AD 100, but some theories suggest that many of its traditions go back to the very earliest times. In the case of Luke (like Matthew, probably to be dated around AD 75), there is a possibility that an earlier version, called by scholars Proto Luke, existed. If so, it could be earlier than Mark's Gospel (AD 65). There is so much uncertainty that it is impossible to construct a table of the order and dates of writing of Bible books with any confidence.

Thought-prompters

1 A few books contain major dating clues. Read Amos 1:1 and see ways people have used to date this book.

2 In a Bible passage we are used to hearing at Christmas we may not have noticed now carefully Luke tries to date events (Luke 2:1,2). If we look at the beginning of chapter 3 we can see him going to even more trouble to do this. Can you think of reasons why the author is so keen to give such details?

3 Some might say a Gospel written later than the others could turn out to be far more accurate. For what reasons might this be true?

14 Were the writers biased?

Sometimes people say accusingly of the Bible that the people who wrote it were biased. This is absolutely true! They were Jews, Christians, or Jewish Christians who passionately believed that God was active, had a message for their time, and that somehow they were part of the process of delivering that message. So they were biased. But all writing or teaching has some bias. You will approach the Gospels as a Christian reader, or an agnostic, or atheist, or member of a faith other than Christianity; it's all bias. That is, you bring with you beliefs and disbeliefs and attitudes before you even open the book. We are all like that. Nobody approaches the Gospels or any question about religion with a so-called open mind, as if they were absolutely objective, absolutely neutral. Moreover, this isn't some peculiar problem that applies to the study of religion. It affects the writing and teaching of history and the theories and practice of science as well. All history is told from a particular point of view. All science is conducted from a set of pre-suppositions. Someone from Britain, which remained free during the Second World War, and someone from France, which had been occupied, would write different histories of the conflict. A modern member of the minority Nazi group in Germany would write a history differently from the way in which a non-Nazi German would write it. Someone alive at the time would bring freshness and personal memories; someone writing who wasn't born at the time might bring information from wider sources. So we all carry some bias, and so did the Bible writers. It is easy to recognise Luke's bias towards the poor and to women, and Matthew's to events that link up with the Hebrew Bible/Old Testament. But it is important to understand bias. First, we have to know our own, so that we can come to terms with it and, if necessary, compensate for it. If we know we are extremely sceptical about, say, miracles, we need to examine the evidence all the more carefully. We can be so busy taking into account somebody else's bias, like the bias of the Gospel writers, that we forget our own.

It is also important to be aware that evidence with bias is not necessarily inaccurate. That the Gospels are by Christians doesn't make them unreliable. Just because the books of the Old Testament were written in the first place by and for Jews doesn't mean they are of no value or use to non-Jews. Just because some of the books about the Second World War are by people who were in it, on one side or the other, doesn't mean they aren't worth reading. Coming to terms with bias in ourselves and the books or newspapers we read matters. Many people still read newspapers without ever realising that they present views that are politically 'left' or 'right'. Whatever the leader of the political party we don't like says is not automatically wrong, but we may not listen long enough to realise that. The most dangerous people are those who genuinely believe that they have no bias at all.

Thought-prompters

1 Think about the main newspapers. Which are to the right politically and which are to the left? Try getting some copies of these papers, preferably for the same day or week, and by comparing them see if you can detect differences in views or outlook. Clue: look at the editorial as well as the reporting.

2 How far do you agree with the statement that the most dangerous people are those who genuinely believe that they have no bias at all?

15 Were the writers eyewitnesses?

When we ask that question we are probably assuming that eyewitness evidence is best. But it can sometimes get confused, so that eyewitness evidence isn't always an automatic recommendation. Think of the last time you were together with a group of people engaged in some activity. Imagine each person afterwards writing an account of the event at which you were all present. How did the event start? What did you see and hear and in what order? Who said what? How did people respond? Who moved where during the first ten minutes? Now suppose you are able to compare notes with others present. If you are reading this with a group try the exercise. Even with my questions to prompt memory I doubt whether accounts will be identical, and some of the written accounts may be very different. You may even wonder whether you were in the same room as some of the other people.

So while we shall explore further the question of whether the Bible writers were eyewitnesses it is more important to focus on the real question: were the writers reliable? I knew someone who had fought in terrible conditions in one of the Allied landings in Italy. He eagerly read each history book about the battle afterwards and if his particular beach landing and his particular platoon were not mentioned he concluded the book was obviously no good. Was this a valid judgement? Accounts of sports matches by players can be similar: 'We were robbed!' 'The ref couldn't possibly have seen.'

Luke tried to gather together accounts and sift them (Luke 1:1–4). That is surely a reliable method. Paul, who didn't meet Jesus in his lifetime, lists and discusses resurrection evidence in 1 Corinthians 15. In Galatians 1:20 he becomes irritated that his reliability might be challenged: 'What I write is true. God knows that I am not lying!' John Mark may have made a modest appearance in his own Gospel in 14:51,52. Tradition has it that he got his information from Peter and wrote it down accurately, but not in order. The Christians who met at his mother's house must have been a source of information and stimulus for him, so perhaps this is an example of a person who was not a witness to many of the events described nevertheless presenting reliable material.

On Matthew and John, opinion is divided. They may have been disciples, as some scholars hold, and if so some personal memories will appear in their Gospels. But if they were not the disciples of those names it does not destroy the importance or reliability of their account, which has to be judged by other means. One theory holds that the gospel evidence came from the disciples and their disciples and friends. It is important to realise that there were more than 12 followers around Jesus. Luke has it that on one occasion at least there were 70 and he also records that groups of women followed Jesus too. There was also Jesus' family, which appears at points in the Gospels, eg Mark 3:31–35. There were plenty of people to talk to about Jesus in the early days. Some travelled to spread Christianity. It is easy to see how the Gospel material was handed down.

A different way of approaching the evidence suggests that, in the earliest times, the sayings of Jesus were passed on reliably by word of mouth and taught to new Christians almost like proverbs or times tables in some primary schools. Narratives were told based on a catchy sentence, which was the crucial part, and these helped people to remember them. These circulated separately (except for the death–resurrection narratives) among the Christian community. It is claimed that evidence for this can be found in, say, Mark, where most incidents seem to have a key phrase as they are told: 'Come with me, and I will teach you to catch people...' (Mark 1:17); 'My son, your sins are forgiven...' (2:5); 'The Sabbath was made for the good of humankind; humankind was not made for the Sabbath...' (2:27); 'How can Satan drive out Satan?' (3:23); 'Listen, then, if you have ears!' (4:9), etc. The narratives were told around these phrases, which were accurately remembered from Jesus' lifetime. In favour of this view is that Mark's Gospel in particular appears on occasions to preserve the exact Aramaic words of Jesus, eg *'Talitha, koum'* (5:41), *'Ephphatha'* (7:34), *'Eloi, Eloi, lema sabachthani?'* (15:34). At the same time accounts (probably written) of Jesus' arrest, sentencing, death, and resurrection circulated. From these, goes the theory, the Gospel writers wove their complex stories that fitted their presentation of who Jesus was. More evidence for this view can be found in the narrative of the woman caught in the act of adultery. In some Gospel manuscripts this appears in John 8:1–11, in others at John 21:24, in one after John 7:36, and in others after Luke 21:38. It could be argued that this is a fine example of a story that had been circulating orally and was almost missed out of the Gospel accounts, except that scribes who knew it tried to squeeze it in where they thought it fitted best. It would be interesting to know whether many narratives were lost in this way, because they didn't have a generally accepted place in the Gospel text.

But this is one view, and it conflicts with the view that the Gospel writers were eyewitnesses or that they knew the disciples, because, if so, why did they need to write down these separate units? On the other hand it is possible to over-emphasise the differences in the two theories. They both agree that what we are reading in the pages of the Gospels, for different but equally valid reasons, can take us back into the words and times of Jesus himself. This is either because the information was routed through the apostles and the wider group of followers, or because from earliest times it had been preserved in catchy phrases taken from the words of Jesus himself. Certainly when the first written accounts were circulating there would be people around who had been there at the time – and plenty of others who had received first-hand reports from them, ready to challenge any significant inaccuracies.

Christian tradition in the second century AD refers a lot to 'the words of the Lord' and it is assumed that there was an oral tradition of Jesus' sayings and teaching that was widely known among the community. If it is not a fake, the Gospel of Thomas would be one example of this. How much of this was ever written down is impossible to say. One can imagine a point so far from the life of Jesus that what was not written down was lost. Possibly another interesting example of this is in Acts 20:35. Paul, one of the great leaders of the Christians, is making a farewell speech to leaders of the Christians in Ephesus, in what is now Turkey. In the course of this speech he quotes words of Jesus: 'There is more happiness in giving than in receiving.' None of the Gospels include these words, and unless this speech had quoted them they would be lost. Much of Jesus' teaching must have disappeared like this sentence very nearly did.

To investigate further

1 Skim read Mark 7:24 – 8:26. Can you spot any catchy phrases that might have helped Christians to remember the stories?
a) What words would you use to describe the way in which the account is written: exciting, boring, common sense, etc? Why?
b) Why does it seem to be an eyewitness account?
c) Are there any details in the account that suggest the writer was present?

2 Read Matthew 5:13–16. Then consider:
a) What do these sayings resemble in English?
b) What do you think these particular sayings mean?
c) Time how long it takes you to remember them.

3 Read Proverbs 17:1–5 and consider:
a) Do you think the method of teaching is similar here to the Matthew passage?
b) Time how long it takes you to learn this passage.
c) Do you think teaching in this way is effective? Why? Why not?

Thought-prompters

The account of the shipwreck in Acts 27:1 – 28:2 appears to be by someone who was present. Read it and consider:

a) how well they tell the story;

b) how the writer might have felt about the events afterwards;

c) what this account shows about travel in the ancient world.

Part Three

Whose Bible is it anyway?

16 Which faiths lay claim to the Bible?

The book that is known to Westerners as the Bible comprises the Bible or sacred writings of two faiths: Christianity and its parent, Judaism (the Jewish faith). That is not to say that the two Bibles are identical. Jews have as their Bible what Christians call the Old Testament. In Judaism it is known as the *Tanakh*. The word is really TNK and is an abbreviation for the three sections within it:

   the Torah or Teaching (T)
   the *Nebi'im* or Prophets, religious spokespeople (N)
   the *Kethubim* or Writings (K)

In the Hebrew Bible these books remain in their original Hebrew language, which many Jews learn as children so that they can read the Scripture in its original and understand it when they hear it read at home and in synagogues. In traditional or Orthodox synagogues Hebrew is still the language for most of the service. In liberal or Reform synagogues the local language plays a much larger part. The books of the *Tanakh* are all the books that Christians call the Old Testament, but arranged in a different order (see page 23).

Jesus was Jewish. He would have used the Torah and the *Nebi'im*, which on at least one occasion he read from a scroll in a synagogue (Luke 4:16–21). For Jesus and his disciples the Hebrew Bible was their Bible. Peter, Stephen, and Paul refer to it as Scripture. The first Christians quoted texts from it that they believed had come true in Jesus. So much of Psalm 22 seemed to apply to him, and much of Isaiah 53, for example. But in the course of time they added their own books and the collection of 27 which is now known as the New Testament grew up. By then Christians weren't Jews but had come in from other religions, and so although the Old Testament was retained, it grew less important to Christianity than the New, which of course contained the recommended reading on the teaching of Jesus and in particular on his death and resurrection.

These books were written in Greek, but even when Greek ceased to be the common language it was never held essential that Christians should learn it to study their Scriptures. Even in the early days translations were made into other languages such as Coptic (a language from Egypt) to help people understand the new faith as it spread. Those Christians who study Greek now in order to study the text more carefully are often students of theology (literally 'word of God'), or training to be priests or ministers.

The Jews do not refer to their Scriptures as the Old Testament, for to them 'old' implies out of date or incomplete. But to Christians the Old has been completed in the New. To Christians the Old still matters, but the New matters more. In the Jewish faith, the New Testament is not used officially at all. Progressive Jews may read parts of it in private reading, though this may not often happen, but the more traditional (Orthodox) Jews will not use it at all. Perhaps it is like a child–parent relationship. The Jewish faith and the Christian faith have the same roots, but the child is different from the parent.

A third faith has a link with the Bible and that is Islam. For Muslims the Bible is not sacred Scripture, although they believe it was originally revealed by Allah. Their Scripture is the Qur'an, in Arabic. But the Bible deals with some of the people whom Muslims regard as prophets, beginning with Prophet Adam. To Muslims, Jews and Christians are 'People of the Book'. The Qur'an also talks about Jesus (as 'Isa) and says more about the Virgin Birth than the New Testament. Together Judaism, Christianity and Islam are 'Abrahamic faiths' that trace themselves back to Abraham (Ibrahim to Muslims) and the promise made to him. There are major differences between these three religions, but it is important to remember their proclamation of One God and their 'sharing' of some of the human ancestors of their faiths.

To investigate further

1 Read Psalm 22 and list the verses which seem to be paralleled in the life of Jesus.

2 Find out about Muslim views of Jesus and identify two things in common with Christian teaching and two important differences.

Thought-prompters

1 In most translations of the Bible the New Testament is published first, followed by the Old several years later. Why do you think this is?

2 Read the account of Philip's encounter with an Ethiopian official in Acts 8:26–40 and consider:

a) What does this passage say about what the prophets' teachings were written on?

b) How did Philip explain the passage?

c) What does verse 32 show about what the writer, Luke, believed was Scripture?

17 Is the Bible used by any other faiths?

The Bible, in the sense of Old and New Testaments, is the Bible or special writing for one faith only, Christianity. No other religion regards that entire Bible as its sacred or special writing though, as we have seen, what Christians call the Old Testament is the complete Bible for Jews. As we have seen, in Islam Jesus is regarded as a prophet or religious spokesman, in the line of Jewish prophets. Although Muslims believe in one God, known to them as Allah, they do not believe that God needs or can have sons or that Jesus was in a special relationship with God, like sonship. To them, he is a prophet among prophets. So although Jesus is mentioned in the Muslim sacred or special writing, the Qur'an, the view taken of him and what is said about him differ considerably from the New Testament picture, not just about who he is, but about the events of his life and especially death.

Jesus himself is viewed with respect not only in Islam, but in Hinduism, Sikhism, the Mazdaznan offshoot of Zoroastrianism, the Baha'i faith and Rastafarianism too. But no members of these faiths go as far as most Christians would in their claims about who Jesus was or his special relationship to God. Nor would they use the Christian Bible as a specially valuable book for their faith. In contrast, what makes the Bible special for Christians is that it deals more completely than other books with who Jesus was, and not just with his teaching (which can be admired in other faiths) but with his death and resurrection. For Christians the Bible is a unique book, or collection of books, dealing with a unique person. Put another way, unlike the view of Islam, the Christian view is that the real revelation is not a book, but a person, Jesus Christ.

To investigate further

1 Find out more about one of the following: the Qur'an, the Guru Granth Sahib, the Avesta, the Upanishads or the Tripitaka. Compare the origin of the book you have chosen with the origin of the Bible and compare the contents of the two books.

2 Imagine a Christian talking to a member of another faith. What might be the main points raised about the Bible and its importance?

18 How Jewish is the Bible?

Sometimes Christians have lost sight of the Jewishness of the Bible. In a few cases they have tried to remove it altogether. Marcion, the controversial Christian who produced an early list of approved books (approved by him!), cut out the Old Testament altogether. In the Germany of the Nazi Reich, the Old Testament was played down. The neglect of Old Testament studies had been growing for some time in German universities before the Nazis came to power. It is significant that the Barmen Declaration, a statement from Christians in Germany opposed to what was being done in their name, had as its first clause:

> Jesus Christ, as he is testified to us in Holy Scripture, is the one Word of God which we have to hear, and which we have to trust and obey in life and death.

They did not say the New Testament, but stuck to the older Christian view that the Bible is to Christians one story. The first Christians were Jews and the Old Testament was their Bible, as it was the Bible of Jesus. They would not have willingly dispensed with it. The books of the New Testament are saturated with references to the Old, as any glance at cross-references or Bible footnotes will show. But the Bible is also concerned with non-Jews – not just the New Testament, but the Old in books like Jonah and in some psalms such as Psalm 87. It is not that, as some Christians wrongly say, the God of the Old Testament is different from the God of the New. Jesus never criticised the God of the Old Testament, his God. Moreover, even in the Old Testament God is shown to be a loving and forgiving God. The book of Hosea testifies to that, but many references in the hymns (psalms), in Jeremiah, and elsewhere support this. It was the early Christian view that this same God sent Jesus.

So the Bible has a strong Jewish element, but not in a sectarian way that makes it unsuitable for non-Jews. What this does mean is that in some cases background knowledge is necessary to understand particular ideas or customs. Those writers concerned with non-Jews realised this themselves and tried to help their readers. Mark explains what is meant by the Jewish custom of *Corban*, something his non-Jewish readers would not have known (Mark 7:11). But in some cases we need to do the finding out for ourselves. Not many people who read the story of Jesus before the High Priest realise the meaning of him tearing his cloak. The High Priest tore his robes and said, 'We don't need any more witnesses! You just heard his blasphemy!' (Matthew 26:65). It is sometimes assumed that he was excessively angry, out of control of himself, and tore his robes out of anger or vexation. In fact this was a ritual legal action in a case of blasphemy. The same piece of the robe was torn and perhaps re-stitched for the next time, though the Mishnah, a collection of non-biblical Jewish teaching, forbids re-sewing. This custom was rather like the British tradition that judges used to wear a black cap on top of their wig when they were about to pass sentence of death. This example is small and relatively unimportant, but it shows that any serious attempt to study the Bible will require information about the Jewish religion: its beliefs, customs, and worship. Some of the customs survive to the present day. We can't de-Judaise the Bible and expect to understand it.

To investigate further

1 Read Psalm 87. How does it show the writer's view that God cared for all nations?

2 What Jewish custom does Mark explain for his readers in Mark 15:42,43?

3 What belief is explained in John 19:31 for the benefit of the reader?

4 Mark refers back to Daniel 9:27 in Mark 13:14. What special clue does he give the reader?

5 What teaching of Jesus did Matthew stress in Matthew 5:17–20?

Thought-prompter

'A Christianity that loses its Jewish roots soon ceases to be Christian.' What do you think this statement means? Do you agree with it?

19 How is the Bible used in Jewish worship?

The scrolls of the religious law or Torah are kept in synagogues in a cabinet called the ark. In Hebrew, ark means cabinet or box. This is often richly decorated and placed in a central position, facing Jerusalem, site of the now destroyed temple. The reading of the Torah scroll and not the sermon or some other activity is the chief point of Jewish worship. It is read on a lectionary basis; that is, a certain passage is laid down for each *Shabbat* (Sabbath). Before it is read, the scroll is removed from the ark and processed round the synagogue, during which people may bow towards it or touch it with their prayer shawls as a sign of respect. It is finally carried up to the platform or *bimah*. The covers are removed, along with the bells that symbolise its sweet sound, and the breastplate like the one worn by the high priest at the temple. The silver pointer or *yad* (Hebrew for 'hand') is held ready to indicate the place in the text for the reading. Readers are drawn from a rota. Some like to read near a special anniversary; perhaps a birth, marriage, or death of a loved one. In the more traditional (Orthodox) synagogues, the readers will all be adult males, aged 13 plus. In more liberal synagogues women and girls over 12 may read. Reading from the law for the first time in public is part of the initiation into religious adulthood. For boys this takes place at the age of 13 when they are *bar mitzvah*, literally 'a son of the commandment', and the responsibility for keeping the law passes to them. During the synagogue service nearest to their birthday they read aloud the passage they will have carefully practised, watched by their proud family and friends, and listen to a sermon by the rabbi about their new adult responsibilities. The reading can be quite an ordeal. Often the text is chanted. Always it is unpointed (see below). The synagogue may be packed. But mostly it is not so much an ordeal as a time of personal and family rejoicing and a major event in the life of the youngster. A party often follows the service. Progressive and Reform synagogues have a similar ceremony for girls who become *bat mitzvah*: a daughter of the law, at the age of 12.

Whoever is reading the scroll in the synagogue will be reading an unpointed text, that is a text without vowels, so they will have first studied Hebrew for some time in order to do this without mistakes. The scroll is often chanted or intoned, rather than read aloud like any book. The reader follows the line from right to left using the *yad* as a pointer. At the end of the reading, the Torah is carefully wrapped up and put back into the ark. Copies are still hand written, on parchment, and any scribe making a mistake in copying has to start again. This calls for concentration, particularly on the last few lines!

Readings from the Prophets and the Writings can be used as well as, but not instead of, the Torah, though a minimum of ten male adult Jews, known as a *minyan*, is required for a full Torah reading and service. The

Prophets and Writings are used without the same degree of ritual as the Torah because they are not viewed so highly. They are scripture, but perhaps comparable to the rest of the New Testament as compared to the Gospels for Christians. The Torah's importance is recognised in other ways in the synagogue. Often the Ten Commandments are written in Hebrew in an abbreviated form on symbolic tablets placed over the ark. *Mezuzot* (singular: *mezuzah*) are small boxes fastened to door posts, which contain the *Shema* (a verse which means 'Hear! Hear O Israel, the Lord, the Lord our God, is one.' These words are found in Deuteronomy 6:4 and are variously translated. Jesus quoted them with approval in Mark 12:29). The *Shema* or other Torah prayers may be contained in *tephillin*. These are boxes worn on the forehead and arm and contain prayers. This is done to keep the instruction in Deuteronomy 6:6–9 about the commandments:

> *Never forget these commands ... Teach them to your children. Repeat them when you are at home and when you are away, when you are resting and when you are working. Tie them on your arms and wear them on your foreheads as a reminder. Write them on the door-posts of your houses and on your gates.*

Jews, like Christians, believe that their Bible is honoured in the keeping, not just in the reading.

Thought-prompters

1 Read Exodus 20:1–17 and consider:
a) What are these rules known as?
b) How important do you think they are for Jews and Christians today?
c) Would you consider any of them to be out of date?

2 Why do you think reading the Torah matters more than the sermon in Jewish worship?

3 Do Christians ever wear reminders of their beliefs or do the homes of some Christians contain reminders? What sorts of things are worn or used?

4 Think of one advantage and one disadvantage of the Torah being read in Hebrew in the synagogue service.

20 How is the Bible used in Christian worship?

Christian worship is very varied. Not only are there lots of denominations – it is estimated that there are about 550 in the UK alone and many more in the USA – but there are many different styles of worship. The Bible is used in all of them and is one of the uniting factors between them.

In some church buildings the Bible will probably be in an obvious place on a lectern or stand at the front (east end). The stand may be a brass eagle, thought by some to represent the taking of the Gospel into the world. In some services the Bible may be carried in procession at the start of the service and the congregation may stand in respect. It is a sign that the Bible is at the heart of the act of worship that is starting

It is common to read an Old Testament passage, or part of a letter, and also a section from a Gospel. As a sign of respect for the importance of the gospel, some congregations stand for this reading and a sermon may follow, to explain or develop the ideas in the Gospel. But if it is a communion service, and such services are now the main services of many churches, the communion itself is partly based on accounts of the last supper of Jesus with his disciples. His words then about the bread and the wine will be quoted, as will Paul's account of it from 1 Corinthians 11, written around AD 53–55, and therefore earlier than the Gospel accounts. In other words, not only is the Bible used in the service, but the service itself has been derived from the Bible.

In some services at the Gospel reading, the Bible may be kissed by the priest as a sign of respect. Candle-bearing assistants or acolytes may flank it on each side as a sign of the light being brought to the world. In many churches, the weekly readings are based on a lectionary (such as the *Revised Common Lectionary*, published by Church House Publishing), that is a set list for each Sunday that ensures that during the course of one or two years all main parts of the Bible are read. These lectionaries relate the readings to the time of the church year – Advent, Lent, Epiphany etc. A Christian who was at worship on most Sundays for the period would hear the most important parts of the Bible read and preached about. In churches not using a lectionary approach, the minister or preacher is free to choose which passages will be read on any Sunday.

At several points in the act of worship, a biblical passage is likely to be read. The reader may introduce the passage with the words: 'Hear the

Word of God as it is written in the fifth chapter of...' These words reflect the hope that God will speak through the reading and preaching to the hearts and minds of the gathered congregation. In some churches the reading ends with a response like this:

Reader: This is the Word of the Lord.
Congregation: Thanks be to God.

The readings chosen will almost certainly link into the theme of the service and the hymns and the sermon.

Some congregations provide pew or seat copies of the Bible so that the congregation can follow the reading or the sermon or exposition of the passage as it is being given. When the reading is from a lectionary, the Bible references may be printed on the service sheet or church notice sheet so that the members of the congregation can study the passages at home in the week following the service they have attended. In that way the impact of the reading can live on, and the hope is that the worshippers will be helped in the week following the service to think about what has gone on and use it in their personal spiritual lives.

In some congregations there may be a Bible text displayed on the wall behind the preacher. Outside, a notice board known as a wayside pulpit may contain on its posters a verse from the Bible for passers-by to read and reflect on. Sometimes it may display an eye-catching and humorous caption, based on a concept or passage from the Bible.

In meetings with no appointed priest or preacher and no pre-arranged service, such as those conducted by the Religious Society of Friends (Quakers) or some Brethren groups, the Bible will still be present on the table in the centre of the meeting. Anyone moved to read from it privately or to read a passage to the whole meeting may do so. Here, whatever is read will not have been planned or prepared in advance, but it will have been 'given' to the reader in the silence as a living message to the worshipping group.

Thought-prompters

1 Why do you think some people are given a Bible for a baptism or confirmation present?

2 What Bible reading would you expect to hear if you were in church on:
a) Good Friday?
b) Epiphany?
c) Easter Day?

3 Some pulpit or lectern Bibles have been given by friends and family in memory of a former member of a congregation who has died. Why do you think this is done?

4 Why do you think some churches keep an open Bible on the altar or communion table, facing the congregation, even though no one reads from it during the service?

21 Are the Old Testament and the New Testament contradictory?

From early times some Christians have been dismissive of the Old Testament and quite willing to drop it from recommended reading. Others have gone further and said they find no common ground between God as shown in the Old Testament and the God revealed by Jesus in the New. Is the God of the Egyptian plagues the God of love? The rabbis had a saying that God was the God of the Egyptians as well as of the Hebrews. But as we have already seen Jesus was a Jew. His God was the God of the Old Testament and the Old Testament was his Bible. The New Testament has the same God and, to Christians, the continuation of the same story. God's love was already known in books like Hosea and Jeremiah. The problem of suffering was known to the writers of Isaiah, Jeremiah, and Job. Christians saw both fulfilled in Jesus.

Of course, many ideas about the world and the way we interpret what happens to us have changed. Illness is not now generally reckoned to be a punishment for sin. If it rains until there are floods we don't usually see God as the cause, but look to the weather forecaster to explain what is happening. Most Christians would not usually see God as directly responsible for natural disasters, yet at the time the Old Testament events were recorded it would have surprised no one for nature to be interrupted in this way (see Exodus 7–12). Few would believe that it was God's will to kill captured prisoners (see 1 Samuel 15) or that it is against God's will to eat rabbits, while it is all right to eat sheep (see Leviticus 11).

Many Christians would point out that in calling God *Abba* (see NIV translation of Mark 14:36), literally 'Daddy', the small child's term for its father, expressing closeness and trust, Jesus was adding a dimension to the developing of understanding of God which went further than the Old Testament. But he never went back on the Old Testament understanding and teaching about God. For all his closeness, God was still God, nor is

Jesus' God 'soft'. He will forgive us, 'as we forgive the wrongs that others have done to us' (Matthew 6:12). Many Christians believe there's a threat as well as a promise in that: God will judge us 'in the same way' in which we judge others (Matthew 7:1,2). He makes demands of his people in the New Testament as well as in the Old. It is the Old Testament God who commands us to love our neighbours like we love ourselves (Leviticus 19:18).

But the New Testament understands God's chosen people to be a wider group than just the Jews, and although the idea can be traced back to the Old Testament (especially in the book of Jonah), it is developed more fully in the New. There, the Christian groups think of themselves as a New Israel, the inheritors of the promises in the Old Testament and the spiritual siblings and successors of the Jews, who are of course invited to join, or remain in, the wider group. None of this means that the New Testament contradicts the Old, but it does take it further and extends some of the ideas of the Old. Often Jesus takes a theme that is present in the Old Testament and develops it. For instance, when examining the religious law in the section of Matthew's Gospel known as the Sermon on the Mount (chapters 5–7). We read, 'You have heard that it was said, "An eye for an eye and a tooth for a tooth." But now I tell you: do not take revenge on someone who wrongs you. If anyone slaps you on the right cheek, let him slap your left cheek too' (5:38,39). Now, contrary to what many people assume, the principle of 'An eye for an eye and a tooth for a tooth' was intended as an act of mercy meant to limit punishment. Jesus takes the same principle further and says do not take revenge at all – even if this involves the risk of being hurt again.

There are, then, differences in the way in which some things are understood in the Old and New Testaments – just as there are differences between the way Christians today and Christians in, say, 1066 and previous cultures would understand things. Attitudes toward the Third World are a good example of this. Christians in the nineteenth century thought of slavery in quite a different way from those before them. But taking everything into account there is a great deal in common between the Old and New Testaments. The New Testament is rooted in the Old. Its phrases, quotations, ways of thinking are full of Old Testament references. Many Christians see the New Testament completing and crowning the Old, making its dreams and visions come true. The better one understands the Old Testament, the better one will understand the New.

To investigate further

Read the parable of the three servants, sometimes misleadingly called the parable of the talents (Matthew 25:14–30). The theme of this is accountability to God. Can you see why the third servant got into trouble? The give-away line is verse 24. What does this parable suggest about God?

Thought-prompters

1 If you tried to sum up Christian ideas about God, what would you say? How far could you back your ideas from passages in the Bible or in the teaching of Jesus?

2 If Christians and Jews worship the same God, what are the real differences between them?

22 How is the Bible used in modern society?

The Bible is not only found in the homes of Christians and in churches. Anyone going to court to give evidence or to be a member of a jury will be given a copy of the New Testament to hold and asked to take an oath, a solemn religious promise, that they are telling the truth. Members of faiths other than Christianity will be permitted to take the oath using a copy of their own Scriptures. The law also allows people the right not to take a religious oath, but instead to 'affirm', that is to make a solemn statement, but without reference to God. This allows for agnostics or atheists to opt out if they wish, though it is interesting to note that the right to affirm was won not by atheists but by Quakers. As a Christian group they objected to the swearing of oaths for two reasons. One was that to take a solemn oath to tell the truth implies that you might not be truthful for the rest of the time. Quakers were known for their absolute honesty, which at times must have made them look rather rude to outsiders ('Do you like my new clothes?' 'No'). The other reason for not swearing religious oaths was that they believed that Jesus himself taught against oaths and that, to put it another way, the Bible forbids its use in these words:

> Do not use any vow when you make a promise. Do not swear by heaven, because it is God's throne; nor by earth, because it is the resting place for his feet; not by Jerusalem, for it is the city of the great King. Do not even swear by your head, because you cannot make a single hair white or black. Just say 'Yes' or 'No' – anything else you say comes from the Evil One.

(Matthew 5.34–37)

Despite what looks to be clear teaching from Jesus, the custom of swearing (in the religious sense) goes on daily in the courts.

It is also easy to find Bibles in hotels, hospitals, or prisons, often in bedside cabinets. Many of these Bibles have been presented by the Gideons. They take their name from a Jewish religious hero or 'judge' (not a judge in the sense of law courts) described in Judges 6–8. The Gideon organisation now is an international association of Christian business people from different churches or denominations, who fund the giving of Bibles in this way in the hope that they will help people. The group was founded in the USA in 1899. Its British branch dates from 1950. There are Gideons in 80 countries and approximately 70 million Bibles have been placed. Perhaps when people are in some sort of crisis, or if they are simply bored with time on their hands, they may open the Bible and read it with care. That is the Gideon hope. Their Bibles have a section that tries to pick out helpful passages for particular times in one's personal life, eg times of anxiety. Sometimes Gideons visit schools to present copies of the New Testament to pupils willing to receive them.

The Bible is found in almost all bookshops, many newsagents and some supermarkets, in a variety of versions and covers, hardback and paperback. Much art has taken a biblical scene or a biblical idea as its inspiration. Music has often taken its inspiration from the Bible, not just in the obvious hymns (though most of these are full of references from the Bible) but also in religious opera or oratorio, which is performed without costumes or sets. Haydn's *Creation* and Handel's *Messiah* are regularly performed. 'The heavens are telling' from *Creation* and the Hallelujah chorus along with 'Unto us a child is born' from the *Messiah* are some of the best-known pieces of music. They have succeeded not in a short time, like a pop record, but over centuries. So has Mendelssohn's *Elijah*, Walton's *Belshazzar's Feast* and various famous Requiem Mass settings. Their popular appeal may vary, but they have endured as serious music. Having said that, many Christmas carols began life as the pop music of their day and survived over many more centuries. Carols for Advent, for Christmas, and for Easter, have predictably used Bible stories and themes. The Bible has also influenced many orchestral pieces. In more modern times Bible themes and stories have made very popular musicals: *Joseph and the Amazing Technicolor Dreamcoat, Jonah Man Jazz, Jesus Christ Superstar, Godspell*, 'Pie Jesu' (pronounced Pee-eh, not pie) from a Requiem Mass etc.

The same is true for art. For nearly two thousand years paintings and sculpture have used scenes from the Bible for their inspiration – lots of artists have painted Moses with the Ten Commandments, the Last Supper, Judas betraying Jesus, the Crucifixion, and many other well-known Bible scenes. But what they have done mainly is to try to paint not the equivalent of a photograph but to put into the painting their reaction to or interpretation of the events they are describing. So one famous Crucifixion, by Grünewald, shows the horror and decay of death in the tortured dead body on the cross. Others show a more serene-looking Jesus, more in control of his destiny. These pictures are around us in museums and galleries, but also in every parish church, in Roman Catholic and Orthodox churches, and sometimes as reproductions in Bibles. But it isn't just that Bible events influence art. It's the Bible themes of hope, love, resurrection, hell, heaven etc that have themselves provided ideas and inspiration for artists, who have taken them into abstract art as well.

Another area affected by the Bible is the English language. From the Bible have come many phrases that are widely used. Their origin is not always known to the users. Here are some examples:

his face fell
gospel truth
a Job's comforter
a Jeremiah
forbidden fruit
a scarlet woman
the sheep and the goats
rule them with a rod of iron
pearls before swine
a Judas
spare the rod and spoil the child
the spirit is willing but the flesh is weak
the powers that be
eat, drink and be merry
the straight and narrow

A concordance will help you track down these phrases in the Bible. These are just a few examples. Can you think of others? Many people do not connect the Samaritans, internationally known for their help to depressed, lonely, or suicidal people, with the Samaritan in Jesus' story, who went out of his way to help a traditional enemy, a Jew (Luke 10:25–37).

To investigate further

1 Where is your nearest statue or stained-glass window showing a Bible scene? What is it of? Why do you think this scene was chosen?

2 Listen to a piece of music, old or new, inspired by the Bible and read the corresponding Bible passage. Then compare the two. What aspects of the Bible passage has the composer emphasised in the music? How far has the composer helped you appreciate something about the Bible that you may not have done otherwise?

3 Consider how many things the Bible teaches are made known to people through Christmas carols. What beliefs are included besides the events of the Christmas narrative?

23 Does every religion have its own 'Bible'?

Most religions have special books or collections of books, sometimes known as Scriptures. These books have common themes in the sense that they often deal with the life of the founder of that religion, how the religion began, and the main teachings of the faith. There the likeness ends, because the contents of the books and the religious teachings in them are not the same, nor are the views on how they came into existence.

It is important to note, for instance, that the Qur'an is a very different sort of book from the Bible. For one thing the Qur'an is one book, not 66. It has 114 *suras* or chapters, arranged from the longest to the shortest. It is believed by Muslims to have been dictated by the angel Gabriel as a result of a series of visions that Prophet Muhammad had when he was 40, round about the year AD 610 (though Muslims have a different calendar). The word Qur'an means 'recitation' and this is another difference from the Christian Bible. According to the standard or official Muslim view this book was revealed via Gabriel from Allah: Muhammad didn't write it or make it up; he repeated what he had been told. He was an agent in the transmission process that ended after his death, when the Qur'an was collected into book form by Caliph Abu Bakr, one of his successors. Muslims learn Arabic, the language in which the words were recorded, in order to read the Qur'an. To them, to translate it into another language risks tampering with, or diluting, the essential message.

In contrast, the Christian Bible has always been seen as a collection of books, whose human origins are more or less traceable, written by different authors at different times. Indeed, all 66 books were written over a very long period of time and much of the material in them was passed on by word of mouth before it was written down. While these writers no doubt saw themselves as doing God's work, little of the Bible, with a few notable exceptions, comes directly from visions. As we saw on page 20, dotted throughout the books of the prophets is the phrase 'the Lord says'. We noted that this seems to refer to a particularly deep or direct inspiration. If pressed further, Christians may well have different understandings of exactly how God spoke. But most Christians, like most Jews but unlike Muslims, would say that as a general principle their Scriptures did not come to be recorded by supernatural means, though of course they do deal with the supernatural – much of what they describe is not bound by the normal laws of nature. In short, most Christians see God or the Holy Spirit at work through the process of human authorship, rather than by supernatural intervention, as is claimed for the Qur'an. For Christians, translation into modern languages is seen as a continuing part of their human responsibility in using communication skills that God has given.

The Sikh Guru Granth Sahib is a collection including teaching from several faiths, but also the poems and songs of Guru Nanak, the founder of Sikhism. Every page in every copy is the same – in other words page 45 in one copy is the same as page 45 in every other copy, unlike the Bible, in which page numbers vary. Sikhs wash, remove their shoes, cover their heads, and bow when they come into the presence of the Guru Granth Sahib. It – strictly, 'he' – is treated like an emperor, even to the point of being reverently put to bed each night. Hinduism had no founders and its sacred writings are stories, often not history, that have been passed down for thousands of years in the ancient language Sanskrit. Nineteenth and twentieth century 'new religious movements' have their special books. The Book of Mormon claims to have been revealed to Joseph Smith by an angel on the basis of gold plates buried under a hill in Manchester, New York State, USA. Mary Baker Eddy, the founder of Christian Science, wrote *Science and Health: A Key to the Scriptures*. L. Ron Hubbard, the founder of the Scientology cult, brought it to notice with his book, *Dianetics*.

Many faiths and cults, many books. What makes the Bible different for Christians is that it is a witness to a living human experience that is still going on (Christianity), that it is the only detailed record of Jesus, and that it is the best surviving record available of others. Because Christians believe that God has spoken uniquely in Jesus, for them the Bible is unique among scriptures. Christians believe that God, by his Spirit, can help people to understand what is written. No other book would be acceptable to Christians as having the status of Scripture.

To investigate further

Find out more about the Scriptures of one other faith and then make a list of differences from the Bible. The list might include such things as the contents of the books, the appearance of the books, the origin and language of the books, how respect is shown to them, how they are used in worship etc.

Part Four

How did the Bible reach us?

24 What were the originals written on?

Writers now use word processors because they can edit and improve the text on screen. It is not so long ago, however, that writers used typewriters to help with speed and presentation and it is not much more than a hundred years ago since some manuscripts were sent to the publishers handwritten. So when we identify the Bible books as originally handwritten we are referring to a method of writing books that people moved away from relatively recently. The modern writer may use a word processor and then post the disc or send e-copy to the publisher. It may be only at the final printing stage that the book appears on paper. This too is a very recent change in the history of the human race.

Some of the Old Testament books may have been written originally on papyrus. Papyrus Is a reed plant, whose name probably comes from Egypt where much of it was grown and then made into a writing material. To do this the reed is sliced downwards into long, thin strips and then beaten and pressed with strips at right-angles to one another; in other words placed like the lines in a noughts and crosses game. When it had dried out it was polished into a smooth writing surface using shaped stone or wooden tools. It rolled easily, so 'books' were rolled rather than closed, and the length of sheets varied. Papyri could be joined together using an overlap and pasting the sheets. If something was shorter than a single sheet of papyrus, for example a business letter, it was cut out of the larger sheet to save papyrus. Contrary to what some books say, papyrus was not vastly expensive in its day and it was hard-wearing. It yellowed with age, whereas when new it was white, but it did not deteriorate rapidly in other ways. It is possible to buy small samples of papyrus now, but watch out, because what is sold to tourists in some countries as papyrus is actually made from dried banana leaves. These rot away soon after tourists have returned home and cannot claim their money back.

Reed pens with ends like small chisels were first used until the Greeks introduced quill pens. In some cases pens were cut and then the end was chewed to make a fine brush. Others were slit to make a nib. Ezekiel saw a man with a writing kit (the GNB translates this as 'something to write with'), mentioned in Ezekiel 9:2. It may have been rather like a wooden pen case of today, but containing a penknife (in those days it really was a knife for making pens), several pens, inks made from red ochre or black carbon and a cloth to serve as blotting paper. Texts that survive show they were using red and black as writing colours. The ink was made from carbon (soot) mixed with thin gum. It was sometimes made into dry tablets for storage and water was added to make it write again, rather like a child's box of watercolour paint now needs the tablets wetting to make them workable.

For major and permanent writings of a relatively short length, stone or clay tablets or wooden writing boards were used. Jeremiah's iron pen (Jeremiah 17:1) might have been for writing on metal. The Ten Commandments were written on stone (Exodus 24:12). We often forget that this form of writing still exists on gravestones. The purpose is exactly the same – to produce something visible and lasting. But that's about as far as the advantages go, since stone lacks portability!

The Jews preferred their synagogue copies of the Torah (religious law) to be written on treated animal skin rather than papyrus. This was an early form of parchment and, later, vellum. The skin was treated by being scraped and rubbed smooth. The skin of young animals was preferred. When sheets were attached to one another they were pasted or stitched. Needless to say, pig skin was never used for this. But animal skin was believed to last longer than papyrus for hard-wearing regular use.

It is thought the New Testament documents were written both on rolls and on codices. Codices (pronounced coe-diss-ease) is a plural word, the singular of which is codex. A codex was made by folding the sheets of papyrus or vellum down the middle and stitching them. It is therefore an early form of book as we know it. Piling them on top of one another and then folding them in the middle meant that the pages were uneven in length. They were trimmed to size. This was done before they were written on. Occasionally, because of the cost of producing papyrus, a roll or codex would be recycled. It would be rubbed smooth again, rather like we might rub out pencil writing of our own, but using tools not rubbers. The resulting text is called a palimpsest, which means 'rubbed smooth again'. With modern detective and scientific work, scholars can sometimes work out what the original text was as well as reading the one written on top, rather like finding a hidden picture under an oil painting.

Even where codices survive only in part, it is possible to work out the number of pages they contained. One, known to us by a reference number, P45, contained all four Gospels and Acts in 220 pages, but only about thirty pages have survived. Gradually codices took over from scrolls as the preferred method of preserving Christian texts. Both sides could be written on and more easily read than on a roll. Rolls also had the disadvantage that when you had finished reading and rolling it from right to left as you did so, the roll had to be rewound to the start. The average length of a roll was 35 feet. Perhaps this made rewinding a job for the slave. The codex was also more convenient for travellers and pages were often numbered. Lines and margins were frequently ruled. Romans were used to parchment notepads and the codex might have seemed to them a natural follow-on. There is a reference to this in 2 Timothy 4:13 where the receiver of the letter is asked to bring the books and 'especially the ones made of parchment'. This is generally believed to refer to these notepads, which were then in common use.

The oldest of the New Testament texts to survive were written without punctuation and in uncials – the capital form of Greek letters. They have no title pages, no division into paragraphs or sections, no illustrations, and no contents pages. They are called uncials, after the capital letters in which they are written. It was not until the ninth century AD that a joined script that helped scribes to write much faster came into use. These later joined scripts are called cursives or miniscules. There were no chapter and verse numbers, but in some a form of paragraphing by spacing exists. Perhaps because of the desire not to waste papyrus, these paragraphs, where they existed, were much longer than our paragraphs.

Thought-prompters

1 What do the difficulties and expense involved in early writing suggest about when and why people might decide to write things down?

2 What problems would the absence of title pages, punctuation, or paragraphing pose for readers?

25 How were the first copies published?

'Publish' simply means to make public. A modern book is published with the help of printed copies, sometimes online copy, advertisements, reviews in the press and complimentary copies. There may be an official launch with author and press present. Ancient books were published, but by an entirely different means. In the first place there was only one handwritten copy. This is now technically referred to as the autograph. This is not because Mark and Paul and others necessarily personally signed them – though Paul sometimes added things in his own handwriting to what his scribe had written for him (eg 2 Thessalonians 3:17) – but because this was the author's own, original, and handwritten copy. Not surprisingly, in no case does an autographed copy of any Bible book survive. But even before printing and word processing, copies could be made quickly. In some cases this would have been done by professional copyists called scribes. The Jews used these for the production of the Hebrew Bible, though they did not use any professional scribe who was around. They used their own Jewish teams and their own methods of checking.

Being a scribe, like most jobs in the ancient world, was a father-to-son occupation. Boys were often apprenticed, to be taught good handwriting, to copy lists and vocabularies, to practise writing from dictation, and also the writing of shorter passages from memory. In some ancient cultures these boys actually had to sit exams in spelling, grammar, calligraphy, accountancy, and technical terms used in the 'industries' which they were destined to work in. There were also oral exams. Education for technology – strikingly modern. Not surprisingly the top scribes became great experts in the field of study in which they worked and this is how Jesus on occasions fell into dispute with 'the scribes', not about the quality of their copying, but about their interpretation of the religious law. Under King David the Chief Scribe was a royal adviser. It was a good job with prospects.

Some scribes sat or knelt on benches with the scroll or codex on a table. Others sat on stools, resting the scroll on their knee. In several ancient cultures there is evidence that scribes also checked their work after they had copied it. In some cases they did not merely copy the words, but kept the same number of words in the same position on the same line, and then checked the line length. Some 'factories' used a production line, with a chief scribe dictating to rows of more junior scribes so that a number of copies were produced at one time. Lines were ruled, sometimes margins were used, and the pinpricks used to mark where to rule are visible on some texts. Occasionally scribes allowed their feelings to come through and they added comments in the margin at the end of a text. These include: 'The end of the book – thanks be to God!' and 'Writing bows one's back, thrusts one's ribs into one's stomach, and creates a general weakness of the body.' One Armenian Gospel manuscript has a note from the scribe to say that there was a snowstorm outside as he was writing, that the ink had frozen, and that his fingers were too numb to write. So scribes were clearly human, and we occasionally see this in their writing.

The rules applying to Torah copying were stricter. It was a rule that the Torah (Jewish religious teaching) had to be copied one copy at a time from another scroll. Until the Romans destroyed the last Jewish Temple in Jerusalem in AD 70 the copies were made from a master copy kept there. Synagogues kept their own copies in a cabinet known as the ark, which faced Jerusalem and often had richly decorated doors. The practice continues to this day. The scrolls were never thrown away when too old to use. Instead they were put into a *genizah* – a sort of sacred bin. This was a place where they could be kept, perhaps used occasionally as practice copies for *bar mitzvah* boys preparing to read in synagogue. The word *genizah* means hiding place. Eventually *genizah* scrolls might be buried very reverently in the ground, as solemnly as if it was the funeral of a person. Sometimes they were just left in the *genizah*. Finding a *genizah* can be a rare archaeological triumph. One found in Cairo in 1890 provided evidence of thousand-year-old texts for scholars to work on. In fact it contained over one hundred thousand fragments, perhaps the world's biggest jigsaw puzzle.

Until Christians started using the Septuagint (LXX) as their Old Testament it, too, was revered in synagogues, but it fell into gradual disfavour among the Jews. The Christian books were produced neither for rich patrons nor for library collections, as many books were. They were written for particular Christian groups, which can be called churches (as long as we remember that they didn't have any church buildings or professional clergy). In the first century AD the Old Testament was still seen as the Scripture for Christians, but each church had letters that had been sent to it, or exchanged with another church (see Colossians 4:16), and may have had its own Gospel or Gospels. Tradition connects the Gospels with particular centres, such as Ephesus in Turkey for John's. It is possible that Mark used parchment notebooks, then in use at Rome, to record his memories of Peter's teaching about Jesus and that he wrote it originally for local circulation among his friends and fellow Christians. Since his Gospel appears to have a missing end (the best manuscripts end at 16:8 in mid-sentence in Greek) it would also fit the theory of a notebook or codex from which the last page had become torn or detached. This is less likely in a roll, where the end would be in the centre, when the roll was rolled up. If, as tradition suggests, Mark went on to become a leader in the church at Alexandria in Egypt, his Gospel would have gone with him and have been copied onto papyrus. If by then, however, the ending was lost and Mark had not come in person, but only his Gospel, it would have been irreplaceable.

In addition to their growing libraries of books, the Christians had 'the words of the Lord', a mysterious oral collection of sayings and teaching. But by the second half of the second century AD the Gospel of John was well known in Egypt, and a fragment of a copy of it dating from then actually survives in the John Rylands Library at Manchester. This is significant, for it means that copies of the Gospel had spread, granted travel conditions of the time, relatively quickly. The lists of approved books called canons are themselves evidence that the New Testament documents were being copied and spread in the second half of the second century. It looks as if codices (paged books) were being used for them rather than rolls. Since the average length of a roll was 35 feet, and it had to be re-rolled after use, the codex must have seemed very convenient by contrast.

Because all the early surviving manuscripts come from Egypt, where the climate was favourable for preserving them, we have to be careful not to over-generalise about how they were written or on what. It might have been different, for example, in Turkey. We just don't have any evidence. Few of the earliest surviving Christian texts show evidence of professional copying, but there would have been literate people able and eager to help in the churches. These early texts have no standard format, which isn't surprising in view of their different origins and copyists. But by the third century there were major Christian centres for study and teaching (at Alexandria, for example) and these centres would almost certainly have taken over the job of copying and making public the texts. The centre at

Caesarea is known to have been using shorthand for some of its texts, and using women scribes. This would have been around the year AD 250.

One scholar suggested that a major set of differences between the Western Text for Luke–Acts and other texts may reflect the writing of two editions: one for sale to sympathetic non-Christians and one for church use. It is possible that different editions could have developed, but there is no hard evidence for this. Another scholar split the Gospel of Mark into what he believed to be passages set for reading in Christian worship. He claimed that these passage divisions account for Mark's order and contents. This too is an interesting possibility that has not been proved. The need to teach the massive numbers of new Christians towards the end of the second century AD may have influenced which texts survived as the best for the job, but since we can't comment on the ones that disappeared, this too is guess work. What is fact is that the major Christian texts established themselves widely and rapidly throughout the growing Christian communities and that although they were not always professionally copied in the early period, Christians took care that the copying was accurate.

Thought-prompters

1 Try to imagine being a scribe in the ancient world, then consider:
a) What parts of the job would give you most satisfaction?
b) What do you think would be the most important skills you would need?
c) Bearing in mind that you didn't retire in the ancient world, what parts of the job would be harder as you grew older?

2 Why does sifting through the findings in a *genizah* matter?

26 How accurate were the copying techniques?

Many of us have relatively poor memories, so people often assume that the ability to remember and pass on information accurately would be equally poor in the ancient world. Therefore, so this line of reasoning goes, what we read in the Bible is likely to have been so changed on its way to us as to be now unreliable. This is a false assumption. Even now there are many Jews who can recite the Torah by heart and the Muslim faith encourages members to learn the entire Qur'an by heart. Many do. Look at the thickness of the Torah or the Qur'an. To enter an Egyptian monastery as a trainee monk in the third century AD, you were expected to know most of the New Testament by heart and you were given an oral examination to see if you qualified. There was no shortage of successful candidates. If we go to a professional secretary who copies documents or takes shorthand, we shall find a very high level of reliability compared to children doing the same exercise. Why? The answer isn't difficult: it is a matter first of training and then of practice. Like learning a musical instrument, the more you practise, the better you become. There is evidence that the professional scribes had both training and lots of practice. We would be wrong to assume they were as bad as we would be.

Several copies of the book of Isaiah were discovered at Qumran as part of the Dead Sea Scrolls find from 1948 onwards. This meant that it was possible to compare that script, copied round about the first century AD, with the oldest surviving script previously known, copied round about AD 895. Until the Dead Sea Scrolls, the oldest surviving manuscripts were codices of the Prophets (Cairo, AD 895, Leningrad AD 916). The oldest manuscript of the whole Old Testament is another codex from Leningrad (AD 1008). The Aleppo Codex (about AD 920) was complete until 1948, when it was damaged in a riot, and about a third of it lost. Comparing the scripts across almost a thousand-year gap means that one can examine how much alteration had occurred over all those years of painstaking copying. There were differences, not surprisingly, but they were few and mainly unimportant. The first Qumran text, known to scholars as 1 QIs.A, led to just 13 altered readings in the Revised Standard Version of the Bible. The Dead Sea finds provided some 500 whole or incomplete books, including 100 Hebrew Old Testament texts. The scribes who kept the Jewish Bible so tightly controlled and carefully copied that there was little alteration, are known as the Masoretes. In Hebrew, *Masorah* means tradition. By AD 100, under the leadership of Rabbi Johanan ben Zakkai they had a standard edition of the Jewish Bible or Old Testament, with notes at the beginning and end of books and in the margins. By then the notes were as tightly controlled as the text. There were Masoretes at work in Babylon and in Tiberias (in Galilee). They used a painstaking checking process. It even included counting how many times each letter of the alphabet appeared in each book, as well as line checks, roll checks, etc. Some texts contain footnotes stating that the book had been checked and found satisfactory. This is a bit like the piece of paper we find inside modern products giving the initial or code number of the checker, in case it is found faulty. There is evidence that they took great care to make sure that the final product was as near perfect a copy as humanly possible. The Masoretes also standardised the system of pointing, the dots and lines added to the text (but above or below it) to give vowel sounds to help pronounce the vowel-less Hebrew text. It is their skill and care in copying the text that is confirmed by the Dead Sea Scrolls, which were not nearly as late in date as the previous Hebrew texts, but were from non-Masoretic sources. Quite a lot of mainly minor mistakes had got into the text before the Masoretes received them. Often the professionals suggested corrections in the margin. Otherwise they did a fine job in passing on the text as they had it.

When we look at the New Testament there are a number of early non-standard copies made by non-professionals, containing quite a lot of minor variations. Small errors in texts might be errors of hearing during dictation. In Greek ai, ei, and e were all similar in pronunciation, like the English e as in ten, and a scribe hearing it dictated might write a wrong letter, just as many school children now write 'of' when they mean 'have'. That is an error of hearing. 'He might of come back late' and 'he might have come back late' can sound almost identical. There are also lapses where a scribe missed a line out because his eye saw an identical phrase a line or two later and he skipped the missing piece by accident. This can happen to people who are reading aloud, where they may miss a line and leap to an identical phrase lower down. The same might happen to anyone copying from a book. Only the photocopier can save us from that as an error of copying. Some scriptoriums (places where hand copies of documents were produced) employed a corrector to check manuscripts as quality control. Their work is identified by different handwriting, by different colour ink, neat crossing out, or sometimes a dot over words that should be cancelled.

What is truly outstanding about the New Testament is the number of copies we have. It has been estimated that there are in total around 13,000 manuscript copies or portions of it. This is many many times more than for any other work of a similar period, eg Julius Caesar's *Gallic Wars* (ten manuscripts), and Plato's *Tetralogies* (seven copies). So although even the best individual New Testament manuscripts may contain quite a number of textual errors, by comparing the oldest and best with one another scholars can get very close indeed to the words the New Testament writers actually wrote. One estimate is that probably over 99 per cent of the New Testament text can be reconstructed.

When we study individual manuscripts it seems that the New Testament scribes may also have made deliberate small alterations to the text. We can compare texts to see how this has happened. They did this to smooth out difficult phrases and perhaps to improve on the one they were copying. Comparing texts suggests that this didn't happen very often and that the alterations, when they did take place, were usually not big ones. Many Bibles have footnotes that show the main text differences so the reader can be aware of them. One example is Matthew 5:22. The main text on the page says:

> But now I tell you: whoever is angry with his brother will be brought to trial, whoever calls his brother 'You good-for-nothing!' will be brought before the Council.

If we look at the footnote at the bottom of the page we read:

> whoever is angry; some manuscripts have whoever without cause is angry.

The first part refers us to the words above and the second part shows the manuscript difference. Perhaps the scribe copying the text thought it was far too hard to say that whoever was angry with his brother would be in trouble. Perhaps he had a brother... So he may have altered it to make it seem more reasonable: Whoever was angry without cause would be in trouble. It is of course possible that Jesus said what the footnote said and that the main text is wrong. But scribes might have altered texts occasionally to smooth them over. It seems unlikely that they would alter one to make it harder to believe and accept. So the detective principle in this sort of work on texts is that in general the harder or more difficult reading of the text is more likely to be original, because late copiers may have wanted to tidy it up or improve it.

Another example of this sort is in Matthew 17:20, where Jesus is explaining to the disciples that it is their lack of faith that has prevented them from curing an epileptic boy. He goes on to say:

> I assure you that if you have faith as big as a mustard seed, you can say to this hill, 'Go from here to there!' and it will go. You could do anything!

We then notice a footnote symbol, and see that some manuscripts add to this the sentence:

> But only prayer and fasting can drive this kind out; nothing else can (see Mark 9:29).

This scribe may have softened Jesus' words, perhaps by referring to methods which he knew were in use among Christians to try to cure illness. Or he may have tried to draw the saying into line with Mark's Gospel, which is generally held to have been written earlier than Matthew and which the scribe may have known. Most New Testament differences are of this level of importance or less. There are few massive differences between manuscripts. One of them is in Mark 16. From early times the best manuscripts ended the Gospel at 16:8, which is actually in mid-sentence. The Greek words read:

They say nothing to anyone. And they were afraid because

English translations tidy up the ending ('because they were afraid'), but it is really mid-sentence. Although a few people are attracted to the thrilling theory that Mark was murdered or died before he could complete the text, most agree that there must have been an accident which destroyed the end of the text before it had been copied. But scribes tried to tidy up the whole ending. Some manuscripts add verses 9–20. This passage appears to summarise the endings in Matthew and Luke in order to round off Mark. Other manuscripts add different verses 9 and 10. Most modern versions print both, explaining that they do not come from the most reliable texts. This level of difference between manuscripts is, however, the exception rather than the rule. The large number of manuscripts available for comparison leads scholars to conclusions such as that drawn by John Robinson. 'When everything has been taken into account the number of variants in the New Testament that make any difference at all (let alone any important difference) to the meaning is extremely small.' Another scholar remarked that if the degree of unwarranted popular scepticism that has been applied to the New Testament texts was applied to other classical texts then we should not be able to say anything with any certainty at all about many classics of history.

Thought-prompters

1 Look at Luke 11:33 and at the footnote manuscript difference. Then consider:
a) Why do you think the manuscript in the footnote tidied up the main text?
b) Why do you think that the main text is more likely to be the original?

2 In a few cases recent discovery of texts means that a numbered verse becomes a footnote. Read Mark 15:21–32 in a modern Bible and then consider:
a) Which verse in older Bibles has become a footnote?
b) Why do you think the scribe added what is now the footnote to the manuscript?
c) Which Isaiah passage might have been in Mark's mind as he wrote verse 28?
d) Why? You will have to read this Isaiah passage to understand this.

27 Can we get back to the text the writer wrote?

One estimate of the earliest New Testament texts to survive is as follows:

85 papyri (every one of these is a codex or book, not a scroll);
268 uncials (the capital letter texts with no punctuation)
2,792 cursives (the texts with smaller, joined up writing)
2,193 lectionaries (these texts are divided into sections for reading in Christian worship)

(from *Introduction to the New Testament* by WG Kummel, SCM Press, 1977)

These numbers are always being revised upwards as new texts are discovered. All the pre-AD-400 texts come from Egypt, where sand and climate helped to preserve them. The texts listed above are all written in Greek. Then there are versions in other languages: Coptic, Armenian, Syriac, and so on. Although these were translated from early Greek texts, they can help us to work out the likely original Greek text . In every case, the original copy of a New Testament book does not survive. The task of trying to work back to what the original said is called textual criticism. Textual criticism doesn't mean being fault-finding, hostile, or unsympathetic to the texts. It is the name given to the careful detective-like comparison of texts to work out the relationship between them and, by studying the differences, to work out the likely original text. It works by probability and not certainty. The exciting part is that new texts are constantly turning up. For example, in 1955 a papyrus now known by its reference number P66 or, after its discoverer, as Bodmer Papyrus 11, was found in Egypt. It contained a copy of the Gospel of John, two thirds of it roughly, from 1:1 to 14:26. Because it can be dated to around the year AD 200 it is a highly important find.

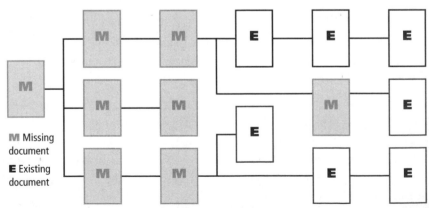

M Missing document
E Existing document

Building up a family tree of documents

When comparing ancient texts, the textual critic works to certain agreed rules. For instance, if a text produces one reading of a verse or phrase and 30 others produce a different one, but the 30 are all the same, it does not mean that the 30 are right and the one is wrong. Twenty-nine of the 30 may turn out to be copies made of one, and the one from which the copies were made may turn out to be not as old as the one that seemed to stand alone. So the one may be nearer the original than the 30. Nor is the oldest text automatically right. Seeing how texts relate to one another and tracing their families is an essential part of the detective work. In some cases the textual critic cannot reconstruct the probable text where the surviving text has been damaged. For example, for 1 Samuel 13:1, many Bibles have a footnote saying that part of the Hebrew text is missing. Taken at face value this could easily result in the surviving text appearing to say that Saul was only a year old when he became king and he was king for two years. This would be nonsense when the next verse goes on to say that he led 3,000 Hebrews out to battle with his son as co-commander. In other cases some reconstruction is possible. Genesis 4:1–16 is the ancient story of Cain and Abel. Verse 8 reads:

> Then Cain said to his brother Abel, 'Let's go out in the fields.' When they were out in the fields, Cain turned on his brother and killed him.

The footnote points out that the Hebrew does not have the words 'Let's go out in the fields'. There is a piece of text missing. Perhaps the scribe, writing at speed, missed them out. But what reasons do we have for thinking that these words or something very like them were in? If we read the whole passage, the sense suggests something like this at this point. But, more important, a study of the Samaritan version of Genesis, also a Hebrew language version, shows that these words are included. So does the Septuagint (LXX), the old Greek version of the Old Testament which was translated from the Hebrew. They could have been tidying up the damaged text they used, but more likely they were translating or copying an older text, now lost, which contained these words. So, like a detective, the textual critic studies handwriting, the links between texts, and needs a good command of ancient languages as well.

Thought-prompters

1 Do you think a particular sort of personality is suited to the work a textual critic might do? Think about or draw up a job description or advertisement to show the sort of qualities needed.

2 Lots of jobs, it is said, require patience. Some people say that patient people make the best school teachers. Presumably the same would be true of textual critics. But do you think patience can be taught? Or do we train ourselves to be patient? Or is it how we are born – genetic patience? Consider the importance of patience in the following situations:

a) in school teaching;

b) in studying the Bible;

c) in doing jigsaws, crosswords, or wordsearches.

28 What are the main texts now used by scholars and translators?

As we have seen, there are thousands of surviving ancient texts, though most of them can be grouped into families which interlink, so there are not thousands of completely different texts. Four main codices are used, along with certain highly important papyrus fragments. One is

Codex Sinaiticus, known by scholars as Aleph, א, the first letter of the Hebrew alphabet, for short. This is written on parchment made of sheep and goatskin, four columns to a page. It was discovered by Constantin Tischendorf (1815–1874), a German scholar, visiting the very remote monastery of St Catherine on Mount Sinai in 1844. You could only enter this monastery by being hauled up in a wicker basket. He noticed that there were sheets of vellum with writing on in a waste basket and that these sheets were being used to feed the fire. Two basketsful had already been burned. He saw some 129 sheets, and persuaded the monks to let him bring away 43 pages of this text. He gave these to the King of Saxony and they were eventually presented to the university library of Leipzig, now in Germany. Tischendorf revisited the monastery in 1853 and to his great disappointment could find no trace of what he had already realised was a vitally important text. He feared that it had been burnt. He made a further visit in 1859 and on the very last evening of his stay he showed the steward of the monastery a copy of his own edition of the Greek Old Testament, the Septuagint (LXX). The steward showed him in response some leaves of the LXX wrapped in cloth and to his surprise and delight Tischendorf realised that he was looking at the leaves he had seen years previously. There were in fact 199 leaves of the Old Testament, a complete New Testament, the letter of Barnabas and Hermas' Shepherd, a well known early Christian book that did not get into the New

Testament. Tischendorf could not persuade the monks to part with this text and so he sat up all night and copied out the text of Barnabas, which had not been seen in full before. The monastery had an offshoot in Cairo. Tischendorf went there and persuaded the head of it to send for the Sinai text. He copied it a page at a time, but was not allowed to keep it or borrow it. At his suggestion the monks gave the remaining 302 pages to the Tsar of Russia in 1862. In return he gave them 9,000 roubles, a very considerable sum of money for that time. The monks subsequently claimed that they were cheated out of it, and there was some scandal, but there is no evidence that cheating had occurred. In 1862 Tischendorf published the codex in full. The Tsar's pages were bought by the British Museum in 1933 for £100,000. They are still there and can be seen by visitors. It is possible that Codex Sinaiticus came from Caesarea originally. Analysis shows that it was written by four scribes and afterwards corrected by six others. It dates from the fourth century AD. Tischendorf saved it from the fire 1,500 years later, but we will never know what else went up the monastery chimney in smoke.

Codex Vaticanus, known for short as B by scholars, takes its name from the Vatican Library in Rome. It has been there since at least 1481 and it contains the best known manuscript of the Septuagint (LXX). It may be related to Codex Sinaiticus and like Sinaiticus is fourth century in origin. It is generally agreed by scholars that this codex along with Sinaiticus together provide us with the most reliable Greek text of the New Testament. The ink on Vaticanus faded slightly and a later scribe went over it, except where he thought mistakes had occurred. He left those bits to fade.

Codex Alexandrinus, known as A by scholars (at least this abbreviation makes immediate sense!), is a fifth-century text, now held in the British Museum in London. The Patriarch of Constantinople, a very important person in the Eastern Church, presented this to King Charles I of England in 1627. The British Museum acquired it by gift in 1757 and it has stayed there since. Three scribes copied this text. They also corrected it, with the help of a fourth scribe who had not been involved in the writing.

Codex Bezae, called D and known to some as the Western Text, is fifth century AD. It was presented to Cambridge University in 1581 by Theodore Beza who had obtained it in 1562 from Lyons, France. It is a puzzling text, because it has a very large number of pieces missing from the Gospels and a very large number of additions to the Acts of the Apostles. It is also damaged and ends at Acts 29:22. Some scholars think it may have come from a second-century Syriac original.

Codex Ephraemi, also called C, is a fifth-century palimpsest – a recycled codex, where the original has been scraped and then written over. In this case it was written over in the twelfth century, with the sermons of St Ephraim replacing the New Testament. Ultraviolet lamps and vidicon cameras mean that palimpsests can be read more easily now, so that it is possible to see the older writing underneath. This is similar to techniques used on paintings that have been painted over.

Of the papyrus fragments the most important are: P45–47, known as the Chester Beatty Papyri. These are third century AD. P66, known as the Bodmer Papyrus, is two thirds of John's Gospel and was written round about AD 200.

In addition to these Greek texts, scholars have available the other-language versions for the New Testament, often made as translations from them, and they have the writings of Christian leaders in the second and third centuries. These people are known as the Church Fathers and their writings sometimes quote sections of the New Testament, often from memory. They provide another ancient source for comparison with surviving texts.

Thought-prompters

1 An Arab shepherd boy throwing stones into cave openings near the Dead Sea discovered the first of the caves containing the Dead Sea Scrolls. The story of their discovery in parts rivals Tischendorf's in adventure and in near misses. It's quite unlikely he would have had any idea that what he found was to become heralded as probably the greatest discovery of documents in modern times. Some have been bitterly disappointed to discover hidden ancient objects only to find they contained old scrolls. Others, like Tischendorf, have been delighted at the same discovery. Why do you think people react so differently? Are there any similarities here with the way people react to the content of the Bible?

2 The idea of scholars working away on the texts listed here seems very remote from everyday life. To whom does it matter apart from them? Why?

29 When did printing come in?

Printing the Bible began in the fifteenth century. A complete Hebrew Bible was printed in Italy in 1488 and a Greek New Testament was printed in 1514 in Spain. This made translation from the two languages easier. We take for granted the massive number of copies of books possible via printing. Small print runs nowadays tend to be 2,000–3,000 copies. Large runs go into hundreds of thousands. Printing had the obvious benefits that you could produce more books more cheaply than with handwritten copies. It also meant your opponents could not destroy your writings as easily, because as long as they could not get hold of the metal plates on which the typeface was laid, you could easily print new copies of the book if they destroyed existing ones. You could also gradually eliminate mistakes. True, there were mistakes – some very famous. In the 'wicked Bible' the printers were fined £300, a lot of money at the time, for missing the word 'not' out of the seventh commandment, 'do not commit adultery, in Exodus 20:14. The resulting text was thought to be someone making a point to the descendants of Henry VIII. In the Vinegar Bible printed in 1717, the chapter heading of Luke 20 was given as the Parable of the Vinegar, and not the Vineyard. The Murderer's Bible, as it was nicknamed, printed in 1795, said 'Let the children first be killed' (Mark 7:27) when it should have printed 'Let the children first be filled'. However, at each new printing the type could be corrected and improved and brought nearer to perfection. That's like the difference between a modern word processor and copying. Every time you copy something you make mistakes and you need to check carefully and correct them. Mistakes will also be made as you type on a word processor, but each time the file is loaded, you can correct mistakes without making more. So the document constantly improves.

Printing also greatly extended the possibility of owning a Bible and therefore of studying it for oneself. William Caxton (1422?–91) is credited with bringing printing to England. He learnt it on the continent and was printing in Bruges in Belgium in 1474 and in England by 1476. William Tyndale and Myles Coverdale printed Protestant English Bibles (1526 and 1535 respectively). These English translations took the Bible (in Latin) out of the control of the clergy and gave it to the people to read for themselves. For his trouble, Tyndale was strangled and burnt at the stake in 1536. But 84 per cent of his New Testament translation was taken into the Authorised Version (1611). The first printed Roman Catholic

Bible, known as the Douai version, was printed in Rheims, France in 1582 (the New Testament) and completed at Douai in 1610. Interestingly, these printers (like the earlier Protestant Bible translators) included English refugees. English-speaking Jews used the Authorised Version (1611) until Jewish translations appeared from 1785 onwards.

The first printed Bibles were weighty affairs and resemble the big family Bibles that are still passed down in some families today. But as techniques of paper making improved it became possible to use India paper, a tough, thin paper, which meant that relatively slim Bibles could be produced. Smaller type made this possible too. Printing has also brought the possibility of cheaper illustrations by reproducing wood engravings, line drawings, colour photographs, and even cartoons of the sort produced by Annie Vallotton for the Good News Bible. Type does not now need to be sorted by hand and placed in trays. Computers have again speeded up production processes. Already, you can buy the Bible as software or read it online: you can call up a book, chapter, verse, or a person or incident from the Bible.

Thought-prompters

1 Do you think it likely that most Bibles this century will be read on screen rather than on paper? Why? Why not?

2 Should Christians learn Hebrew and Greek like Muslims learn Arabic?

30 Where did the chapters and verses come from?

It surprises some people that the writers of the Bible didn't put their own chapters and verses in. These are for reference, to help find passages quickly, and were added later. Just as there were various and different lists of approved books, there have been different systems for reference in the Bible, which were standardised relatively lately into the one we now use. Codex Alexandrinus (generally referred to as A) contains chapter divisions and headings called *titloi* in Greek. Codex Vaticanus (generally referred to as B) has section divisions that relate to breaks in the sense: there are 62 in Mark's Gospel, 152 in Luke, 170 in Matthew, and 80 in John. Our present chapter divisions were introduced into the Vulgate Latin Bible by Stephen Langton (died 1228) in his time at the University of Paris. He later became Archbishop of Canterbury and was on the barons' side against King John at the time of the Magna Charta.

Robert Estienne (1503–1559), a Paris printer, who like so many people involved in Bible translation or printing had to flee from persecution, introduced the verse divisions now in use, when he was a refugee in Geneva, Switzerland in 1551. This was in a Latin and Greek New Testament. The first New Testament in English to contain these verse divisions was the Geneva Version of 1560. Legend has it that the numbering was done in a moving carriage. This might account for uneven verse length, mid-sentence division in some cases, and a general impression of lack of planning, but there is no firm evidence to support the legend. The Old Testament is similar. Various systems existed which were eventually standardised. Numbering was added after verse divisions had been in existence for some time. Dots previously marked verse divisions. So the New Testament writers can only quote or refer to Old Testament passages by referring to the book they are from, or the passage, eg 'the passage about the bush', which refers to Moses and the burning bush: Exodus 3. Verse divisions in the Old Testament existed from the early days of Christianity. These were standardised but not numbered by the Masoretes in about the year AD 900. Hugh of St Cher introduced chapter divisions in 1244. Numbered verses were introduced by Rabbi Isaac Nathan in about 1440.

To investigate further

Choose at random a two-page section of the Old Testament and a two-page section of the New Testament.
a) How far do the verse divisions occur at sentence ends?
b) How far do the verse divisions make sense, linked to the meaning of the passage?
c) How far are the verses roughly of the same length.
d) How far do the chapter divisions show the natural ends of stories or sections?

Thought-prompter

Can you identify one advantage and one disadvantage of starting again with a completely new splitting up of chapters and verses to make more sense than the accepted ones?

31 Where did the bits in the margin come from?

Many Bibles contain what might seem to be rather puzzling notes, sometimes at the bottom of the page and sometimes in the margin.

Sometimes there are so many and full of numbers that it looks almost as if a page of maths has somehow got mixed up in the section you are trying to read. Other Bibles have very few of these references. There are different sorts of margin or footnotes. How many are used depends on the particular Bible. A Bible produced for academic study will obviously have a lot more than a pocket Bible designed for lightness and easy reading. Here are some of the sorts of things that may be found in margins and footnotes. Let's imagine we were reading the Gospel of Matthew in, say, the GNB, and were in the middle of chapter 4. The first we might notice are the references below the heading 'Jesus begins his work in Galilee'. We find that there are references to sections in two other Gospels. This sort of reference is provided to tell the reader that another Gospel version of the same narrative can be found by looking up the passage listed. This means that an interested reader could compare the passage and note any interesting differences or similarities. If we look at the bottom of the page, there are more references. Next to 4:12 we see Mt 14:3; Mk 6:17; Lk 3:19–20. These are not references to the same narrative told in other Gospels, but references in this Gospel and others to a related event. In this particular case, it is the imprisonment of John the Baptist, which is mentioned in Matthew 4:12.

Another useful function of these margin references is to point to an important saying or event in the Old Testament that may be being referred to or even quoted in the passage, of which the reader may be unaware. So in verse 10 when Jesus says 'The scripture says ...' the footnote shows us where we can look up his quote: Deuteronomy 6:13. A footnote suggests that Jesus might have had in mind Psalm 37:11: 'the humble will possess the land and enjoy prosperity and peace' when he said 'Happy are those who are humble; they will receive what God has promised' (Matthew 5:5).

Some modern Bibles have inserts intended to help the reader, sometimes indicated in a different colour print or a different font such as italic. These may add geographical detail or brief comment on ancient custom referred to in the text.

Footnotes may be included to show the reader an important alternative way of translating a passage (see Jesus' words to Judas – Matthew 26:50) or an important difference in Greek manuscripts (eg Mark 6:22, about who exactly Herodias was). Alternatively, they may provide brief historical notes for the reader, as in the same passage (Mark 6:14–29).

The footnote helpfully explains which 'King Herod' is being referred to – not the one of the Bethlehem toddler massacre, but another, Herod Antipas – and the note also corrects his title to tetrarch or ruler. So it pays the reader to keep an eye on margins, inserts and footnotes: they can add important details and understanding to the passage being read.

Thought-prompters

1 How much would you want to take the number and detail of margin and footnote references into account if you were buying a Bible for yourself for personal reading?

2 Read Mark 16 in a modern Bible version with margin references and/or footnotes. What surprises do they provide for you about the ending of this Gospel?

3 Read John 1:1–23 in a Bible with footnotes and/or margin references and check every reference. How far do you think they helped your understanding of the passage?

Part Five

How was the Bible translated?

32 Where does Latin come in?

At the time of the Apostles, Greek was the common language spoken throughout the Roman empire. Latin was the official language. It was used in the law courts, in official writings, and by educated people. As the Roman empire spread into Europe and strengthened, Latin spread and began to displace Greek as the common language. It also displaced some of the ancient languages of conquered countries, as it did in Gaul (France) and Spain. It was not surprising, therefore, to find a growing demand for Latin versions of the Christian books in the third century AD. Various translations were made, but in AD 382 Pope Damasus commissioned one of the most widely travelled and clever Christians of his time, Jerome, to produce a Latin Bible and thereby end the big differences that then existed between the Latin texts. Jerome did this, and it took him from AD 390 to 405, while he was living at Bethlehem. He did not merely study the existing Latin texts, but went back to the Hebrew and Greek in order to produce a better translation. His text is known as the Vulgate, from the Latin word *vulgata*, meaning 'in common use'. It is related to our word vulgar, which has come to mean common in the bad sense; low, in poor taste. That was not its meaning in the Vulgate. Jerome used chapter headings. It is a sign of the low importance he attached to the Apocrypha that although his careful revision and translation of the Old and New Testaments took 15 years, he rushed through the Apocrypha in a matter of months. As with so many new translations in the history of the church, Jerome's was attacked strongly. It was said that it was too different, that it had changed the basic meaning, that it was unsuitable. Behind some of this, of course, lay the dislike that some people have for anything they're not used to or haven't grown up with. Nevertheless, Jerome's Vulgate Bible became very widely accepted in the church and at the time of the Council of Trent (1545) was commended to Roman Catholics as the only suitable version. It was already more than a thousand years old and the ruling that it had to be used unfortunately prevented any translation direct from the Hebrew or Greek for the Roman Catholic Church for centuries. Even a more recent English version by R A Knox (New Testament 1945, Old 1949) was a translation from the Vulgate. Having to work like this built in two sets of mistakes – the mistakes from Hebrew or Greek into the Latin of the Vulgate and then the mistakes from the Latin into the English. Better Greek and Hebrew texts than the ones Jerome had used had meanwhile been discovered. Some translators got round this problem by 'consulting' the Hebrew and Greek when they translated the Vulgate. Now, the ruling no longer applies and one of the most recent Bibles to be produced by Roman Catholic scholars, the New Jerusalem Bible, goes back to the best available Hebrew and Greek texts.

For these reasons, therefore, for centuries the Bible in use in the English church was in Latin. Few people hearing it would have understood it, and for many Bible education would largely consist of reading the stories in stained-glass windows or in wall paintings in churches. These were like the comics of the time, telling the story in pictures. The mystery plays (not crime thrillers, but mystery in the technical sense of the mystery, or unexplainable reality of Jesus, God as man) also told Bible stories in the language of the time. English examples survive from Chester, Wakefield and York, where they are still enacted regularly. These performances are attended by visitors from all over the UK and abroad. But what have become high points for York visitors were once the bread-and-butter experience of local people. They provided actors and audiences for these plays, which set out all the chief Bible stories and Christian teaching at a time when the Latin Bible was closed to most English-speaking people. Only gradually, and only in bits, did English translations arise.

Soon after AD 700 the hymns (Psalms) of the Old Testament were translated by Aldhelm, Bishop of Sherborne, Dorset. The famous scholar-monk Bede, in Jarrow in the North-East, translated part of the New Testament and was working on a translation of John's Gospel around the time of his death on 25 May, 735. King Alfred of burnt-cake legend (871–901), in reality a very clever man, translated some psalms and Exodus 21–23. The Wessex Gospels had the Gospels in Old English (pre-1066 Conquest language) in the tenth century. The Norman Conquest of England brought about a lot of changes, including language. It led to the rise of what is now called Middle English. The Ormulum, by a monk called Orm, was a translation of the Gospels and Acts, followed by metrical (ie in verses) psalms. During all this time, the monasteries and convents were producing copies of the Vulgate. But even there, some of the nuns and monks and many of the lay brothers, knew no Latin. By the end of the fourteenth century English versions were in use in some of the monasteries for the main New Testament letters, Acts, and for the early part of Matthew's Gospel, which was then believed to have been the first of the Gospels to be written. They were also using a summary of Old Testament history. But there was still no English Bible and there was still no people's Bible because the translations were for monastery use. Twelfth-century Latin ruled.

Thought-prompter

If we had only church stained glass to rely on for information about the Bible, what passages would we know most about and what would we know least?

33 Why did translation into English cause arguments?

It seems strange in today's society to think that there was strong opposition to the idea that the Bible should be translated into English and therefore made available to ordinary people. It was this consequence that made some resist the idea. They thought that ignorant people reading the Bible would get all sorts of unsettling ideas that might lead them to attack life as it was, a way of life that kept so many in poverty and a few in extreme luxury. It was thought that the peasants might actually resort to violence if they became dissatisfied with their position in life. The belief was that a little learning is a dangerous thing. Moreover, some of the first translators seemed to be controversial and rebellious people.

John Wycliffe (1329–1384) was one of them. He was once Master of Balliol College, Oxford, but lived at Lutterworth, Leicestershire till his death. He believed very passionately that the Bible should be the rule for faith for Christians. Everyone should obey the Bible, he believed. He assumed that everyone would interpret the Bible as he did, which did not of course follow. But how could everyone obey the Bible if they couldn't read it? Learning to read was hard enough, without having to learn to read a foreign language (Latin) at the same time. He wanted a people's Bible. Wycliffe also attacked the power and corruption of the church of his time. He taught that it was not right for the church to be involved in state matters or to own vast possessions and property. After 1378 he questioned the authority of the Pope, the current doctrine of the Mass (Communion) and the abuses of the right of sanctuary, which provided shelter in churches for criminals. He and his travelling preachers, who were known as Lollards, must have seemed very threatening with their criticisms of the church. It may be that some of the people involved in the Peasants' Revolt (1381) saw him as an inspiration. None of this would help the church establishment to welcome his idea of an English Bible for English people. The first version of his Bible was made between 1380 and 1384 and the second was made after his death. Although it is referred to as Wycliffe's Bible, it was in fact translated by his supporters and friends. He inspired it, rather than did it himself. It was still hand-copied. But he and his followers were so politically suspect that their translation was not welcomed either. Lollards were persecuted by burnings and the last remnant, among the poor people of the Midlands, disappeared in the early 1400s. In 1408 it was forbidden, on penalty of death, to make English translations of the Bible. Surprisingly, English versions spread, though as translations from the Vulgate they contained double mistakes.

The name of William Tyndale (1494?–1536) is well known in the story of the English Bible. After studying at Oxford and Cambridge he was a private tutor in a household at Old Sodbury near Bath, but after a period in London was obliged to go abroad to escape persecution. The 1408 law still applied. He produced a New Testament translation in 1526 that was printed. He revised it in 1534, adding warnings about pirate texts and their alleged improvements to his original, which had made it worse. It is interesting to note copyright and pirate problems long before DVDs, computer games, downloading software and so on made this a well-known modern problem. Tyndale produced a translation of the Pentateuch in 1530. He had gone to live in the safe city of Antwerp (now in Belgium) but he was kidnapped from there by his enemies – he too had attacked the power of some priests – and imprisoned under harsh conditions. He asked if he could finish his translation of the Old Testament in prison but it is unlikely that this was permitted and he was brought to trial for heresy (teaching against the beliefs of the church) and executed. It is curious that as this trial and execution were being carried out, copies of his New Testament were circulating in England, the country he had fled as unsafe. His New Testament had a significant influence on the Authorised Version of the Bible, produced in 1611. Tyndale produced a translation that was direct and forceful in its language, thus making it accessible to his readers. It is clear to read even now. Printing also made it affordable. Early copies cost between 7 and 12 groats (13p and 20p) each, within the price range that labourers could afford.

The first complete Bible printed in English was produced by Myles Coverdale (1488–1569). He too suffered from changing political fortunes and was exiled three times. At one time he was Bishop of Exeter but was deposed when Mary Tudor came to power. Coverdale didn't know Greek or Hebrew, so he had to rely on other translations, probably Tyndale's, but also some German ones and the Latin Bible, the Vulgate. He used chapter summaries of up to a paragraph in length. His 1535 edition was followed by a 1537 edition under royal licence. It was one text that led to the production of the Great Bible in 1539, a copy of which was placed by law in each parish church. But the translation that has been in use the longest forms the subject of the next section. This is known as the Authorised Version.

Thought-prompters

1 'Printing is unstoppable. Whether it's good or bad, pornography or Bibles, you can't stop it spreading.' How far is this true?

2 It is hard for us to imagine how someone must have felt, being able to read the Bible in their own language for the first time. Try, however, and consider:
a) What did it give them that stained glass, wall-paintings, and plays didn't?
b) Which books do you think they would have read first? Why?
c) Do you think that in a way, the church authorities were right, and that the Bible would give the people something with which to judge the church?

34 Where did all the 'Thee's and 'Thou's come from?

Some people still associate the Bible in English with out-of-date language, with 'Thee's and 'Thou's and 'begat's and 'begotten's. They have at the back of their minds the Authorised Version (AV) of 1611, also known as the King James Version, a version which dominated the English Bible scene until last century and which is still in use. By its admirers it is thought of as beautiful language to glorify God, the language of Shakespeare, who incidentally was alive in 1611. Like Shakespeare, it has some sense of prose rhythm about it. By its critics it is seen as incomprehensible and based on inferior Greek texts which have left it with translation errors. One small Bible society, the Trinitarian Bible Society, exists to promote the AV text only.

In 1604 King James I commissioned a new version of the Bible. He was personally involved in planning it, and took an active interest in the work. He established six panels totalling 47 men to translate it. Three panels worked on the Old Testament, two on the New Testament and one on the Apocrypha. They met in Oxford (two panels), Cambridge (two), and Westminster (two). Most of the leading Bible scholars of the time were involved and they were paid very little! A draft version was then revised by a smaller group of 12 men, two from each contributing panel. It contained chapter headings, some cross references, and paragraph marks. Curiously, these cease at Acts 20:36. It has been suggested that the printer ran out of the signs used. If a word was necessary to complete the meaning in English, but was not part of the original Greek or Hebrew, it was added in distinctive type: italic in modern printings of this version. So if we use the AV we must not assume the italics are there for emphasis. This Bible was dedicated to the king but it was never officially appointed to be read in churches. It is sometimes known as the King James Version. It is important to remember that the language used by this translation was once modern English. It is changes in the way in which English is spoken and written, and the discovery of more reliable Greek manuscripts, that have made it out of date.

In 1611 'Thou' was singular and 'You' was plural, like *tu* and *vous* in French. This was everyday speech. Connected with Thou was Thy or Thine (= your) and Thee (= you as object, eg 'If thou hittest me, I shall hit thee!'). The AV didn't invent this language; it took it from daily use of the time. As these forms of speech died out in everyday conversation except in dialect like the Yorkshire 'tha', for some readers their difference emphasised God's difference, beauty, and majesty. They preferred Thou as a way of addressing God in prayers and felt You was too familiar, like saying 'Hello, Mate' to God. Other readers felt that modern times call for modern words.

Thought-prompter

Read 1 Corinthians 13 in an AV Bible and then read it in a modern version. Do the same with the Lord's Prayer from Matthew 6:9–13. Which versions do you prefer? Why?

35 Why are new translations still being made?

Language constantly changes its meaning. Today the word overlook means to forget. A hundred years ago it meant to check. So factories would employ an 'overlooker' – not to help people forget things they didn't want to remember, but to supervise. Some phrases from older translations of the Bible are similarly misleading. Solomon's 'outlandish' wives were not necessarily bizarre characters prone to fits of wild and extreme behaviour. They were simply women from other lands. At the time the King James Version of the Bible was translated the word conversation meant what today would be called lifestyle. So when this translation talks about Lot being rescued from 'the filthy conversation of the wicked' it does not mean rescued from a round of dirty jokes but from the actions of evil people.

At the same time, new Hebrew and Greek manuscripts are being found that mean that the accuracy of translations can be improved in the constant effort to get back to the words the first Bible writers wrote. This means that although there are lots of modern versions, there will always be a need for more. Perhaps Christians in this century will need to use three or four versions in their lifetime to keep up to date. Some have already lived through use of the Authorised Version, the Revised Standard Version, the New English Bible, the Good News Bible, the New International Version, the Revised English Bible, the New Jerusalem Bible etc.

But that is only the story of new English translations. The Bible is still being translated into other languages. It is estimated that over 6,000 languages are spoken in the world today. Under 10 per cent of these languages have a complete Bible, more than 10 per cent have a New Testament only, and a further 900 have no full New Testament but at least one Bible book. So the task of first-time translations goes on alongside the task of updating existing translations. A local church may request its national Bible Society for help in producing a translation into the local language. They in turn may ask international Bible Societies to provide expertise and possibly funding as well. In choosing translators, care has to be taken to select people not only highly qualified in Greek or Hebrew, but also in the local language and customs. Some parts of the Bible pose real problems for people who live in quite a different culture or climate from the original hearers – as we see in the next section. Yet the translator has to try to use the common or ordinary language of the day, just as the New Testament originally did.

Thought-prompters

1 Think of one advantage to Christians of using the same version of the Bible for all their life and one advantage of using several different versions.

2 Read Matthew 25:14–30 in the Authorised Version (1611) and then rewrite it into modern English. Compare what you have written with a modern version after you have written it. This exercise will have produced a paraphrase, not a translation. What is the difference between the two?

3 Can you think of any Bible words or ideas that might be hard to translate into other languages and cultures?

a) How far do you think it is difficult for people living in an industrial society to understand the farming world and outlook of much of the Bible?

b) Read the parable of the sower (Mark 4:1–9)

   i) How similar to modern farming are the methods used?

   ii) Do you think Jesus' first hearers would have found it easier to get the point than we do?

36 What are the main current English translations and what are the significant differences between them?

Over the years two basic ways of translating from one language to another have developed. The first way is to concentrate upon translating the exact words used, and the second upon translating the meaning of a passage. In the first approach the ideal is to preserve as much as possible of the form of words and word order from the original language to create what's often called a literal, or formal correspondence, translation. There was a time when most Bible translators favoured this approach 'A vineyard was made to my beloved in horn the Son of Oil' is an early English translation of Isaiah 5:1. It is a direct, and it could be claimed, accurate translation of the Hebrew, but it's not likely to mean much to most English speakers – either now or then. From the seventeenth century until the beginning of the twentieth, formal correspondence (the word-for-word emphasis) was generally accepted as the model for translation. Even the titles of some Bibles left the reader in little doubt as to where the translators had their priorities – 'A modern, correct, and close translation' (Williams 1812) and 'The Greek Testament Englished' (Crickmer 1881).

The Revised Version of 1881 and the American Standard Version of 1901 are perhaps the best known products of this era and were large-scale, conscious attempts to preserve the form of the original language even though the words could not always appear in the same order as the original. To some extent this tradition of translation has continued into more recent times through the Revised Standard Version of 1952 – a translation highly regarded in churches, colleges, and universities – and the New Revised Standard Version of 1989. However, this formal correspondence approach brings its problems. Phrases with the same meaning can differ quite distinctly in form between different languages. For instance, 'What time is it?' in English becomes 'What hour is it?' in French or 'How late is it?' in Dutch. During recent years there has therefore been a general movement away from this method. Today, greater emphasis is given to an approach to translation known as 'dynamic equivalence'.

Rather than word-for-word, dynamic equivalence is a meaning-for-meaning translation. In this approach the ideal result would be for the translator to produce in the new reader (using language B) the same reaction to the text as the original author wished to produce in the first readers (using language A). This means carefully analysing the meaning of words, phrases, and sentences in their original language and reconstructing that meaning using words and expressions that are natural in the language into which the translation is being made. Though widely adopted by the majority of Bible translations in general use today, the principle is by no means a totally new idea. Martin Luther in the sixteenth century said, 'Whoever would speak German must not use Hebrew style. Rather, he [sic] must see to it, once he understands the Hebrew author, that he concentrates on the sense of the text, asking himself, what do the Germans say in such a situation?' However, dynamic equivalence is not a matter of just expressing the general ideas contained in the original text. The whole point of dynamic equivalence is to make it possible for the present-day reader to understand what the original reader must have understood. The circumstances of time, place, and custom must stay firmly the same.

This is not a priority with all translations. Some set out to be cultural paraphrases. British examples have included versions of the Gospels in Scouse and broad Yorkshire dialects. Some have become much loved – —often giving new insight into passages so familiar to some people that the usual translation just floats over them. These paraphrases can be fun to read, but their technique of transposing the events described by the original writers into another time or place, eg Washington DC for Rome , is not part of the dynamic equivalence principle or normal serious translation practice. Cultural differences and fashions in language, however, present problems for all translators. Many translations deliberately set out to avoid them.

Paraphrases have sometimes been produced for young readers. Sometimes the priority is to create a text that can be listened to when read aloud. This was the aim behind the Contemporary English Version, first published as a complete Bible in 1995. Sometimes the difference is more one of presentation than translation. The New Century Bible is also presented as The Youth Bible.

Sometimes Bible users debate which might be 'the best' translation. In short, there is no straightforward answer to the question. It all depends who you are and for what purpose you want to use the Bible. The translation that best suits the university professor won't necessarily go down best in the school classroom or the pub. The question of whether you need difficult words to express difficult ideas is also an area of keen debate. All fresh modern translations use far more, and far earlier, manuscripts to translate from than was possible when earlier English translations were made. Most popular modern translations are undertaken by more than one person and invariably lots of checking and consultation takes place. So we can still legitimately ask which translations are most popular or which translation might help a particular group of people in a particular way, but, when it comes to 'best', everyone will have a different idea of what 'best' means. Some people keep a collection of different translations so that they can compare a passage and see how different versions present it.

To investigate further

Look up the first three verses of the Letter to the Hebrews in several different translations. How many of the issues mentioned in this chapter can you recognise? Which of the versions in front of you do you prefer and what are your reasons? Can you think of a user group who might prefer a different translation?

37 How do modern English translations come about?

In the 1950s Chicago businessman Kenneth Taylor became increasingly aware of the puzzled expressions on his children's faces as he read them passages from the Bible. He was using the King James Version of 1611 – at that time the most commonly used translation. Upon questioning his family about what they had actually understood from what he read he became more and more concerned. So to help children make some sense of the Bible he began to reword passages in simple conversational style. His children liked what they heard. They told others about it and soon there became quite a demand for these understandable Bible readings. Earlier Kenneth Taylor had done a Master of Theology degree and he began to use his skill in producing a written paraphrase of one book of the Bible—most of it done during his daily train journey to the office. Other books followed and in 1962 he formed his own publishing company, named after the Bible translator William Tyndale, to publish and promote *Living Letters*, a paraphrase of the New Testament epistles. This is part of a tradition going back to JB Phillips' work in the 1940s and 1950s. *Letters to Young Churches* was his title for the paperback edition of the New Testament letters. The Living Bible, as the finished treatment of the Taylor Bible became known, sold millions of copies worldwide. A more recent equivalent is *The Message*, a paraphrase by Eugene Peterson, or *Book of Books* by Trevor Dennis, a theologically based paraphrase of selected biblical narratives.

Feeling that existing versions of the Bible don't help all readers to understand what the writer intended, has from time to time led people to think about making a new translation. This is a much more complex operation than that undertaken by Kenneth Taylor. He did not retranslate but paraphrased an existing English Bible. Taking the American Standard Version as his main source, he attempted to say the same thing that he understood earlier translations to be saying – only using different words, ones he thought his children could understand. A new English translation means going back to early Hebrew and Greek manuscripts and translating them into another language: English. This much more extensive task has usually been considered worthwhile in order to make the transfer of thought from the original language to the modern version as direct as possible.

So the story of all major Bible translations begins when Christians feel there is a large demand for some kind of Bible use that is not fully satisfied by existing translations. The second vital stage is for a publisher to invest in a major project that will take several years of work before any copies can be sold. Thirdly, for most translations, teams of translators and consultants need to be brought together.

In 1946 the Annual General Assembly of the Church of Scotland decided to approach other churches in Britain about producing a new Bible translation. The following year representatives of the Church of England, the Church of Scotland, the Free Churches, the British and Foreign Bible Society, the National Bible Society for Scotland, and the University Presses of Oxford and Cambridge met. They organised the translation and production of what appeared in 1961 (New Testament) and 1965 (Old Testament) as The New English Bible. Their system was to use one translator per book to produce a draft copy, which was sent to panel members for revision. They sent it to the literary panel for further revision and the agreed text was then sent to the Joint Committee. This was revised in 1989 as The Revised English Bible. 1966 heralded a new Roman Catholic Bible of major significance, The Jerusalem Bible (English Version). This was inspired by the Dominican School of Biblical Studies in Jerusalem from 1948 onwards. Hebrew and Greek texts, not the Latin Vulgate, were the basis for this, along with references to the French translation that had preceded it. By this time the Second Vatican Council (1962–1965) of the Roman Catholic Church had introduced vast changes, including the changing of the language of the Mass from Latin to whatever the local language was, and warm support for links with Christians from other churches. It is not entirely appropriate to talk from this time onwards of Roman Catholic and Protestant Bibles as separate. Scholars had been working together for a long time, reading one another's books about the manuscripts, and attending conferences together. The Jerusalem text was intended for any serious Bible reader, Roman Catholic or otherwise. It reads well aloud and is used in some Protestant services just as suitably as at Roman Catholic Mass. Christians now would hold that a good translation is good for use anywhere, whatever church it comes from. The Jerusalem Bible was revised in 1985 as The New Jerusalem Bible.

In 1966 the American Bible Society published the New Testament of the Bible in Today's English. The Old Testament followed in 1976. Dr Robert Bratcher coordinated the work of a group of translators and consultants

– both on Bible scholarship and English usage. This translation aimed to produce a version accessible to everyone who could speak English whether as a first or second language. (See previous unit for explanation of the common language principle.) Much careful work and wide consultation was then undertaken to make the language thoroughly natural to British English-speakers for the British edition. In 1976, The Bible Society published this edition as the Good News Bible. An edition containing the Apocrypha/Deuterocanonicals appeared in 1979. Many other editions that include a variety of background notes and photographs have been published since. The success of this translation is indicated by an entry in the *Guinness Book of World Records*. The 1989 edition estimates that between 1976 and 1988 in excess of 104 million copies of Today's English Version (the GNB) were sold worldwide – either as New Testament or as full Bible.

By the mid 1960s it seemed to many Christians that there were quite enough modern translations either recently published or on the way to completion. It was an act of faith in 1965 when a group of Bible scholars meeting in Chicago decided to begin a completely new translation. And it was just as big a risk for the New York International Bible Society when, two years later, they agreed to sponsor the project financially. However, as a result an international group of 100 scholars, under a controlling committee of 15, produced the New International Version (NIV). The New Testament appeared in 1973, followed by the full Bible in 1978. The name New International Version reflects the fact that the committee producing it consisted of distinguished Bible scholars from many English-speaking countries as well as from many different Christian denominations. In the translation itself there is also an emphasis on using English that sounds natural in the different countries in which the language is spoken. The translators deliberately tried to avoid either Americanisms or Anglicisms. So when a British edition was produced few changes, other than British spellings, were needed. The commitment of those involved was fully justified, as today the NIV is a very popular modern translation. It has led to others based on it, like the New International Readers' Version (for children) in 1985, Today's New International Version (with 7 per cent of the original updated and changed) and The Life Application Bible, a version containing devotional insights alongside the text.

For a number of reasons, translations are revised. However careful translators might be, as time goes on some words take on a different meaning or emphasis and some way of translating a phrase may be misunderstood. Minor revisions to some versions go on without most people realising. The Revised Standard Version of 1952 came from the American Standard Version of 1901 and led to the New Revised Standard Version of 1989. Fifty-one might sound a fairly ripe old age for a translation to produce offspring. But that can be easily beaten by another revision. In 1982 the King James Version was the basis for the New King James Version—over 350 years after the original and involving 119 contributors. However, for the first 300 years of the King James Bible, often known as the Authorised Version, there were few alternative English translations. This translation was regarded by many as 'the' English translation. Comparing and revising popular translations is a relatively recent development in the story of the Bible.

The world wide web has brought benefits to Bible students, although some web sites are blatant in their bias for or against particular modern translations and have to be used with care. The Bible Gateway, a site by Nick Hengeveld, allows for a passage or a word to be searched for and compared in 18 versions of the Bible. The Unbound Bible from Biola University, California, allows for comparison of ten English versions alongside Greek and Hebrew, four other ancient versions and 42 other languages. There are other sites, as a web search will reveal.

To investigate further

1 Look at the translators' introduction at the front of several different modern translations.
a) What does it tell you about the aims of the translators?
b) What does it tell you about the methods used?
c) What does it tell you about who commissioned the translation?

2 Look at one of the two Bible web sites mentioned above. What advantages and what disadvantages does it have over 'hard copy' (written text)? Would you choose an online Bible in preference to a printed copy?

38 What sort of problems do modern translators face?

Making new translations of the Bible is always necessary as the worldwide church grows. Often the initiative starts with local Christians who make a request through their churches to a national Bible Society. Sometimes representatives of a translation organisation like the Wycliffe

Bible Translators take the initiative and decide to live among a group of people in order to learn its language and make the Bible available to them. Sometimes translation is part of a government programme of literacy. Wherever possible, new translators will be found to translate into their own language. However, in the case of a previously unwritten language, the first step is for someone to come in from outside – to learn the sounds and work out how to write them down.

Usually, when thinking of any new translation there are political considerations. Can some of the neighbouring peoples read? If so, what kind of writing do they use? Does everyone expect a different political group to be in power before long? If so, have they any known ideas about writing and language? In order to keep things as simple as possible the Latin alphabet, the kind used for the English language, will normally be adopted – along with a few phonetic signs to show how words should be pronounced. However, there may sometimes be strong political reasons why another alphabet, such as Arabic or Chinese, should be used. People are becoming increasingly aware that the type of language and even alphabet we use, says a lot about us. Then there are often geographical and cultural issues that cause problems. Perhaps there is no word for snow in a country that never sees any, or no words for large animals in countries like Papua New Guinea where the largest native animal is the pig. Among the Zanaki of Tanzania the idea of knocking on doors, except by thieves to check if a house is empty, is unknown. The normal way of calling on someone is to stand outside and shout out your name in a loud voice and wait to be asked in. So they would find a straight translation of Revelation 3:20, in which God's messenger stands at the door and knocks, quite confusing. A translator would have to put 'calls' or 'shouts' instead. Another African group in Mali which enjoys a certain type of snake as a treat for a meal would have found a quite different meaning in Matthew 7:9,10: 'Would any of you who are fathers give your son a stone when he asks for bread? Or would you give him a snake when he asks for a fish?' In this case the translator found that they disliked toads as much as many Westerners dislike spiders, so the word 'toad' was put in, instead of snake. In a hot country, on the other hand, 'white as snow' would have to become 'white as cotton'.

Idioms are always an issue in translation. For in all languages there are special ways of saying things which would make no sense at all if translated word for word, eg 'pulling your leg', 'getting the sack' or 'being fired', 'getting plastered', or 'not being able to hold a candle to someone'. The Bible translator is always looking out for the right way of treating the Greek and Hebrew idioms. There is an interesting Old Testament example in the translation of 1 Kings 18:21. The passage tells the story of Elijah and the prophets of Baal on Mount Carmel – Elijah is challenging the people to decide between God and Baal. In the King James Version, Elijah says to the people, 'How long shall ye halt between two opinions?' In the Good News Bible, 'How much longer will it take you to make up your minds?' In Hebrew he says, 'How long will you go limping on two divided things?' According to a well-known Hebrew scholar the 'divided things' were legs, so as well as asking his question Elijah was laughing at the strange dances of the prophets of Baal. The Bengali Bible translates this expression in an interesting way. Here Elijah says, 'How long will you remain with your feet in two boats?' This is used because people in Bengal sometimes come and go between long, dug-out boats tied together to make pontoons or bridges. Anyone who has had one foot on the shore and the other in a boat with the gap growing wider between them, will have a good idea of what it means.

When translations are made for the first time perhaps only one Gospel is attempted and later, if Christian groups grow and demand more, translations are made of the New Testament and then the whole Bible.

Thought-prompters

1 You are sent to a remote area to learn a language that has never been written down. First imagine trying to explain, using sign language only, who you are and what you are trying to do, and then list the main difficulties you might have in writing down a language that had never been written before. Think about languages you have heard spoken and might recognise by their sounds, but which you cannot speak, eg (unless you live in Wales or are Welsh-speaking) use Welsh.

2 You are a translator in a country that used to be part of the British empire but is now independent. The official language of the country is Arabic and there are several local languages. A minority speak English as well as a local language. Many minorities speak the local language they were brought up in and no other. Educated people speak Arabic as well as a local language. Which would you choose for your translation and why? What would be the advantages and disadvantages if you simply recommended the people to learn English and so not need a translation at all?

3 One problem translators face is the use of idiom. Imagine translating these expressions literally into another language:

> I bet he's right; you're looking blue; mind your own business; keep mum; she was a runner up; you've got to stand up and be counted.

4 Sometimes idioms are peculiar to a local area. If a person from some parts of Yorkshire says, 'I'm starved' they rarely mean that they are starving, or even hungry at all. They mean they are cold. What dangers are there in using idioms? Why might idioms pose particular problems to Bible translators?

Part Six

How is the Bible read?

39 What sort of people read the Bible?

All sorts! The *Guinness Book of World Records* estimates that between 1815 and 1975 five billion Bibles were printed. They rank it as the world's best-selling book, with the Qur'an second and the *Guinness Book of World Records* third! The Bible is read by scholars and researchers, but it isn't just for clever people or people studying it for their job or for GCSE Religious Studies ethics sections. Jews and Christians of all ages and levels of intelligence may read it to deepen their understanding of their faith. Curious people may read it simply to see what it's all about. You don't have to be religious to read it. Some parts require patience. Guides and introductions are often very helpful in order to understand it. It is a 2,000-year-old text, and there aren't many books of that age we could reasonably expect to pick up, read, and understand straight away, or without help in the form of a commentary. Yet in the 2003 Biblos survey, 63.1 per cent of the 1,066 young people who took part said that the Bible is important and 65.4 per cent felt it teaches about God. People from all walks of life are found to read it, in all sorts of places – workplace, pub, school, bus etc. Scripture Union has, in partnership, produced material so that people with learning difficulties can access the Bible.

Christians have special reasons for reading the Bible, because it is the record of Jesus and the Book of God – that is God is its main 'character', from Genesis to Revelation. Some Christians attend churches that take Bible teaching seriously and join or form Bible discussion groups. Some Christians read it individually, a section every day, as a sort of spiritual exercise, taking time to think about it and perhaps to pray as well. They see it as a sort of spiritual food – 'daily bread' to quote a Bible phrase. They may use special Bible reading notes to help them and to select the key passages. Some find it easier to do this in a house group setting where members of the group can discuss their particular problems and feelings about a passage and encourage each other with the difficult bits.

Some Christians don't read it daily, but more inspirationally – when they feel a special need or reason.

In all these ways, people read the Bible. But their approach to doing it is sometimes quite different. For some it works best to take a saying or verse and just think about it, over a period of time. Others put themselves into a Bible narrative in their imagination, and try to think how they would have felt, what they might have done, in that situation. Prequels and sequels can be an imaginative way in – you try to think what might have led up to the events in a narrative (prequel) or what might follow (sequel). Sometimes this can be compared with the biblical prequel or sequel, although these are not always provided in the Bible. Another approach preferred by some people is to memorise a short passage. Others may read quite long passages fairly quickly and think about them afterwards.

Thought-prompters

1 If you sat on a bus or train reading a large and noticeable copy of the Bible, how do you think those sitting around you would react? Why? Would you be embarrassed to read it in public in that way? Do you think that behind these possible reactions or embarrassment lie any wrong ideas – for instance, that anyone reading the Bible in public must automatically be deeply religious or that religious belief is somehow embarrassing?

2 Many people assume that the well-known Christmas story comes entirely from the Bible. Read Matthew's and Luke's versions. There is no snow or even any kings at the stable. What other surprises can you find? Where do you think the extra details have come from?

40 Are different interpretations possible?

In a way there will be as many interpretations of the Bible as there are readers. Readers will find different meaning in the same books according to their own questions, beliefs, and interests. If you read a novel it can sometimes come as a surprise to see a film of part of it and how the TV or film producer has interpreted it, or how the individual actors play their parts. The film may even look quite wrong, because in our mind we had seen it in a quite different way. Similarly, no two preachers preaching from a Bible passage will ever see exactly the same meaning in it, as any tour of Easter or Christmas church services would rapidly show. Sermons would be boring if they did. So the message is the same, but readers and preachers interpret it to their own situation and time. This re-interpreting means that the Bible can speak freshly to each generation of Christians. Far from these different interpretations being a nuisance, they are a sign of spiritual vitality. Even the clash between some interpretations can lead to healthy debate between Christians.

Although each individual will interpret the Bible differently, there are broadly similar ways of interpreting it. Not every person understands it completely differently from everyone else. Just as there are different styles for swimming, yet no two people swim exactly alike, so it is with approaching the Bible. It is important to remember that the different ways of interpreting the Bible have grown from within the Christian family and have each, in their own way, tried to help Christians understand it better. These different approaches to the Bible do not correspond to the traditional denominational divisions. In other words, it isn't the case that all Roman Catholics interpret the Bible one way, while Baptists interpret it another way, and Methodists a third way.

The different approaches to the Bible are sometimes labelled by outsiders, using words like literalist, fundamentalist, and radical. These labels are not always helpful, because the people of whom they are used don't always find them suitable and don't always think that they describe their position very fairly. It is best to use these with caution, if at all, or, better, to try to get behind them to what the person is actually saying. There are different approaches, but there is also common ground. We can distinguish a conservative approach, which conserves or sticks closely to the idea that the text of the Bible is reliable history. We can also distinguish a more liberal or freer approach, which is more willing to question the historical accuracy of the text but still stresses its religious truth. These approaches are found in other faiths too. There are Orthodox Jews who are conservative in their approach to the Scriptures and Progressive Jews, whose interpretation of the *Tanakh* (called by Christians the Old Testament) is freer. Of course, some conservatives are more conservative than others and it seems to outsiders that they don't want to accept even the slightest possibility of anything being other than completely matter-of-fact in the way it should be understood. Some liberals are more liberal than others and it seems to outsiders that they are willing to surrender almost the whole of the Bible as history and just accept its high religious ideals or even to disregard it altogether. The great majority of Christians are somewhere between these extremes, however, and the debate goes on.

To investigate further

Talk to two Christians you know about their attitudes to interpreting the Bible. If you get stuck, ask them about the walking on the water and the Virgin Birth as starting points. Have a Bible handy so you can talk to them about particular bits. What are the significant similarities and differences in their approach?

Thought-prompters

1 How far do you think different approaches to Bible interpretation are signs of Christian disunity?

2 How far do you think that outsiders interested in Christianity assume that there is just one way to interpret the Bible? Would more explanation help or confuse them?

3 Is it helpful if a common view of interpreting the Bible prevails within a particular local church or house group?

4 'If even one story in the Bible isn't historically true, you can't believe any of it.' How would you answer that remark?

41 Does God speak through the Bible?

This is really a question about the inspiration and authority of the Bible. The two are connected.

(a) Inspiration

Most Christians would describe the Bible as an inspired book, but what they mean by the word inspired varies. For some, the Bible is inspired because it is inspiring. That is to say, it has had such a powerful effect on the lives of women and men: it has helped to change the direction and purpose of their lives, and through them affected the lives of others. It has inspired them to be Christians, or to be better Christians than they were before. But to many Christians it goes further than this. They would emphasise that the Bible has been inspired by God in a way in which no other book has. They may go on to refer this inspiration either to the contents of the Bible or to the way in which it has been transmitted. We can see these different ways of looking at inspiration in almost any dictionary definition of inspire or inspiration. In Latin the word *spirare* means to breathe and *in* means in! In-spiration is therefore literally breathing in (note how expire means to breathe out and hence has come to mean to die). Breathing life into things and those things becoming living beings is one of the oldest ideas in the Bible and appears in the Genesis creation narrative: 'He breathed life-giving breath into his [that is, Adam's or man's or humankind's] nostrils and the man began to live' (Genesis 2:7). So inspiration was connected with life, the life of the spirit. For some Christians, to say the Bible is inspired is to say it's inspiring not just in the sense that we may say Shakespeare is inspiring, but in the fuller sense that God has, so to speak, breathed God's spirit into it. It represents witness to God and his actions. It gives spiritual life.

As they have developed this idea further, Christians have stressed different things about inspiration. Some have stressed what is known as verbal inspiration. To them every word is as if it had been dictated by the Holy Spirit. It is therefore unthinkable that there could be errors of any kind at all in the Bible. Other Christians prefer to talk about plenary inspiration. They mean that the Bible is inspired by the Spirit in all the subjects it deals with, though not necessarily in the grammar or the sentences or in every tiny detail. Its writers were humans and therefore could make mistakes. They were prompted, excited by their experience of the Holy Spirit and that is what set them off writing. Other Christians talk about the moral inspiration of the Bible, by which they often mean that it is inspired by the Spirit in its religious and moral teaching, but that one would not necessarily turn to it as, say, a definitive or text book source for science. Each of these views brings its problems, as each tries to wrestle with the difficult job of finding words to express how special the Bible is to Christians and how it has been 'breathed into' by God.

(b) Authority

In a society like ours, which places great emphasis on individual freedom, on personal choice, on the individual deciding what to believe and how to behave, external authority is not a very popular idea. It conjures up a picture of being told by some outside agency – in this case, a book – what to do or think. Non-Christians are not likely to be excited about the idea of the Bible as an authoritative book. They may prefer to have the freedom to engage with it simply as literature and ask any question they want.

But Christians choose to accept that the Bible has authority. They claim it as special, different, supremely important – the words used to describe it will vary from person to person. But the word authority comes from author. We have seen that it was never believed that God in person wrote the Bible, but it was certainly believed that God's Spirit inspired the writing.

What this means in detail about the authority of the Bible varies. Here is a selection from Christian history of what different people have said, claiming its authority, at different times:

- It contains all that is necessary for salvation, without needing anything adding (John Wycliffe, 1329–1384, re-stated in Article 6 of the 39 Articles of the Church of England, 1563).
- It is the authority for not baptising infants (Menno Simons, 1496–1561).
- The Bible is Christ's own word of mouth, or the words of the Holy Spirit (Roman Catholic Council of Trent, 1546).
- It is above the authority of the church (Confession of Dositheus, 1672).
- It is a record of human religious experience (Friedrich Schleiermacher, 1768–1834).
- It reveals God's holiness and grace (PT Forsyth, 1848–1921).
- It is the inspired and infallible word of God – Scripture is equivalent to 'God says' (BB Warfield, 1851–1921).
- The Bible is 'God-breathed' but also a humanly written book, which can be explored like other books (Gerrit Berkouwer, using 2 Timothy 3:16).
- The Bible, 'God's written word', is the witness to the event of God's revelation, like capturing a flash of lightning in a photograph (Karl Barth, 1886–1968).
- The gospel is the one source of all saving truth: it is transmitted in two ways, by Christian tradition and by Scripture (Roman Catholic Second Vatican Council, 1965).
- The Bible is the only written word of God, without error in all it affirms, and the only infallible rule of faith and practice (Lausanne Evangelical Christian Covenant 2, 1974).

Different Christian individuals and groups, different views. But what no recognised Christian group can do is to put itself above the Bible, to abandon the Bible. The authority of the Bible is recognised. It is the detail of what this means that leads to debate.

Thought-prompters

1 What books have you read that you would call inspiring? Why?

2 Traditionally, Christians have held that human beings are a complicated mixture of body, mind, and spirit. In this life at least we don't see body, mind, or spirit working separately from one another. We only see body; mind and spirit work through it. To what extent do you believe in the spiritual? Are there people who you would say are more spiritually minded than you? What motivates them? How far does it make sense to talk about the Bible as spiritually inspiring?

3 'The danger of talking about the Bible as an inspired book is that it makes it look unreal, too good to be true, too different from other books.' Do you agree or disagree with this? Why?

4 Ask Christians you know how they would understand the idea of the Bible as inspired.

5 Which of the views about the authority of the Bible described above appeals to you (a) most and (b) least? Why?

6 Should we be questioning the high status given in our society to the authority of the individual? What are the strengths and weaknesses of individualism?

42 Has the Bible affected the lives of its readers?

The Bible has affected the lives of very many of its readers and been a source of comfort or, as we suggested in the last section, inspiration. But in some cases it has had a very remarkable effect on the lives of people hearing it or reading it. Augustine (AD 354–430), who may not be well known even among Christians now, was a very clever man and eventually one of the most significant Christians not only in his own time, but in the whole history of Christianity. He was born in the Roman province of Numidia, now Algeria, and brought up with a non-Christian father and a Christian mother. He quickly abandoned the Christianity of his boyhood. He became professor of rhetoric (the art of public speaking, argument, analysis of ideas) at the University of Milan. In a sense he wanted a religious faith, but found the ones he had tried lacking. At Milan he went to hear the preaching of Bishop Ambrose. But he also enjoyed an adventurous private life and said the prayer: 'Lord, grant me chastity, but not yet!' It was in some distress that he went in search of quietness to think about his religious beliefs and his personal life and was one day in a garden when he heard a child, as it seemed, in the next garden chanting, 'Take it and read! Take it and read!' A book containing the letters of Paul which Augustine had been reading lay nearby and he picked it up quickly, opening it at random. He read these words:

> Let us conduct ourselves properly, as people who live in the light of the day – no orgies or drunkenness, no immorality or indecency, no fighting or jealousy. But take up the weapons of the Lord Jesus Christ, and stop paying attention to your sinful nature and satisfying its desires.

These words were from Paul's letter to the Romans (Romans 13:13). For Augustine they marked a turning point. The phrase 'no orgies or drunkenness' stunned him. It was as if it was addressed directly to him. It marked his conversion to Christianity. Through the effect on him, the effect reached others, for eventually Augustine became a bishop. Far more importantly, he turned his talents to writing books about Christianity. These had a wide influence on Christians and outsiders and the most famous, *The City of God*, is still printed and sold today. Its paperback edition runs to more than 600 pages.

Francis of Assisi (1181–1226) was already actively working for others in helping lepers and in trying to rebuild a ruined church when on 24 February 1208 he went to visit Portiuncula in Italy. While worshipping there he heard these words read in the service:

> Go and preach, 'The Kingdom of heaven is near.' Heal the sick bring the dead back to life, heal those who suffer from dreaded skin diseases, and drive out demons. You have received without paying, so give without being paid.

These words are from Matthew 10:7 onwards. The whole passage, verses 7–19, is worth reading. It changed Francis' life, bringing to the surface ideas and beliefs he had been half-forming for some time. He got rid of his belongings, put on a long dark garment tied with a cord round the waist, and set off as a travelling preacher to help people and to try to save souls. From this beginning arose the Franciscan friars, not monastery-based monks, but travelling preachers, who shared the poverty of the people. The Rule that Francis made for them, really a set of simple rules, was taken from the Gospels.

Martin Luther (1483–1546) underwent a personal experience known as the Tower Experience, somewhere between 1512 and 1515. No single text from the Bible seems to have dominated this experience, but it seemed as if Luther felt suddenly the essential point of the Gospels, that faith alone makes people right with God and not works. In other words he came to the view that no one can do enough good things to make God accept them. It is only our faith that puts us in a right relationship with

God, not a list of good deeds we may have done. That could be countered by a list of bad deeds. He found evidence for this belief in Paul's Letter to the Romans as well. As a result of this man and the ripples he created in the pond of religion, the Reformation of the church began. He translated the Bible into everyday German because he believed that people should be able to read it in their own language and not to have to learn Latin first.

At 8.45 pm on 24 May 1738 Luther's 'Preface to Paul's Letter to the Romans' was being read at a meeting in Aldersgate Street, London, when a man in the audience felt his heart 'strangely warmed' as he later wrote in his journal. This was John Wesley (1703–1791), already a Christian, but from now on a committed preacher who tried to take what he called scriptural holiness to the people, whether they came to church or not. He began to preach in the open air in Bristol in 1739. This was considered very shocking at that time, and in a lifetime he travelled thousands of miles on horseback, time he used to study the New Testament in Greek. He preached an estimated 40,000 sermons and he left 100,000 Methodists after his death, in what has since grown into a major world church.

In recent times one of the famous Christians in the world was Mother Teresa of Calcutta. At a time when many other people would just want to enjoy a restful retirement, her work to care for the uncared-for in India and to raise funds for the purpose made her internationally famous and admired. She was awarded a Nobel Prize for these efforts, but she said in an interview:

> Faith is a gift of God. Without it there would be no life ... Faith in Christ who has said 'I was hungry, I was naked, I was sick, and I was homeless and you cared for me.'

Her work was based on living out these words and they come from the Gospel of Matthew (25:31–46). It is continued today, even after her death.

These are just a few examples of Christians who subsequently became famous. Their stories are also evidence of how one letter only, Paul's to the Romans, at different times in Christian history has had an enormous effect. It is important to remember that although these Christians played a major part in Christianity, the Bible has had an effect on countless Christians who never became famous, but read it, were helped by it – and took action as a result. You may have met some of them.

To investigate further

Find out from a collection of short biographies about the life of any famous Christian who 'came in from outside'. How far did words from the Bible, read by them, or heard from other people or preachers, influence them at the time at which they became Christians or more committed Christians?

Thought-prompters

1 'I suppose I ought to read the Bible every day, but I don't. Over the years I find myself coming back to it in patches, when particular things have happened to me such as depression, or if a relative has died. Sometimes I might read more carefully at home one of the readings from the Sunday service. At other times a Christian festival such as Easter inspires me to read the death and resurrection stories in the Gospels. Reading the birth stories on Christmas Eve makes Christmas more real and helps me to escape from the commercialism of the modern Christmas. The house is all quiet, the shopping has ended, and the excitement and noise of Christmas morning hasn't begun – there's a pause. Sometimes I'll read a Bible book from cover to cover, though if I find it's really given me something to think about, I'd rather stop there and just think, take it in rather than rush on. So when I do read the Bible, I might read a whole book one day, but only one verse the next and nothing the day after.'

a) Do you think this person has been deeply influenced by the Bible? How?

b) How typical do you think this person might be as a Christian?

c) Can you identify one thing this person gains by not reading the Bible every day and one thing that they have lost?

2 Interview a Christian you know about whether they can identify any influence the Bible has had on them, or any particular passage that at a particular time was important or helpful.

43 Has it affected the church?

It is a strange thing that although the church produced the Bible, in a way the Bible produced the church. The church came first, of course, in those early days after the resurrection, before any letters had been written, and before any Gospels were even thought of, when the Bible to Christians meant the Hebrew Bible and when the teachings of Jesus were being passed on by word of mouth. As the collection of documents written by members of the Christian groups or churches and for use within these groups grew, it was the groups who began to produce the lists and it was the church councils that eventually decided on the final list of books for the New Testament. All this makes it look as if the church produced and decided on the Bible. In later centuries, there have been periods when the church was becoming powerful and corrupt, or just formal and lifeless. In such times someone has arrived on the scene to re-form the church on the basis of the Bible, to bring it back to the Bible teaching so that it would live again. Luther reminded Christians that the just would live by faith, not by good deeds or payment of money to buy forgiveness. He based this on Romans 1:17 and chapter 4.

> *As the scripture [Paul means the Old Testament here] says, 'The person who is put right with God through faith shall live.'*

(Romans 1:17)

The result of this and the debate that followed was the reformation of Western Christianity into those churches we group together under the umbrella label Protestant: Lutheran, Anglican, Methodist, United Reformed etc, alongside the Roman Catholic Church (or, in those days, against it).

In England, John Wesley (1703–1791), an Anglican clergyman, was moved to spread 'scriptural holiness' throughout the land. By this was meant a return to Bible faith and teaching; a sense of the world as his parish; a desire to bring outsiders into the Christian church. Wesley's sense of this calling changed his life and led to the formation of the Methodist societies in the Church of England, which take their nickname from their methodical or careful study of the Bible. Shortly after Wesley's death these societies broke away from the Church of England. So was born what has grown into the worldwide group of Methodist churches of today.

At times of persecution, the Bible has been used to strengthen the church or defend it against false teaching. In Nazi Germany when a state-supported Reich Church was being used as one of the Protestant churches to boost pro-Nazi and anti-Jewish Christianity, as if such a thing were possible, it was a group of ministers who banded themselves together in a grouping called the Pastors' Emergency League in 1934. They produced a statement, now known as the Declaration of Barmen, after the town in which it was agreed, attacking the attempt to Nazify Christianity and insisting that its biblical basics should be kept.

Perhaps more controversially, in the twentieth century, in some countries Christians opposed dictatorships. They developed liberation theology, inspired by the events of the Exodus, sometimes physically fighting for freedom and justice and a fairer society, but appealing to the Bible, to the teaching of Jesus, and to the Old Testament prophets for support for their ideals. Some Christians appeal to the letter of the Bible – the exact words. Some appeal to the spirit – the general sense. One case of this was the nineteenth-century campaign against slavery. The Bible doesn't come straight out and condemn slavery. It appears to accept it as part of the social structure of the day. But Christians came increasingly to feel that the idea of slavery was against the very spirit of the Bible and its idea of people. Paul got near to this:

> In the same way, all of us, whether Jews or Gentiles, whether slaves or free, have been baptised into the one body by the same Spirit, and we have all been given the one Spirit to drink.

(1 Corinthians 12:13)

To investigate further

1 Just as the nineteenth century saw Christians seizing on the implications for slavery in the Bible, in the twentieth century people saw the implications for gender equality. That is, the equality of male and female in Christ. This has led to Christian concern for equal opportunities and a Christian basis for anti-sexism.
a) What side would you expect supporters of this view to take in the debate still going on in some churches about the ordination of women?
b) Some Christians would like to remove male language used about God, either by referring to God always as God and never him (or her) or to use female and male words for God so that the Lord's Prayer would become Our Mother-Father in heaven', etc. What do you think about this? If you dislike it, is it simply because such language is unfamiliar?

2 Other Christians, at present a minority, hold that the spirit of the Bible (though clearly not the letter) is inconsistent with eating meat. Animals are seen as part of God's creation and, for instance, battery breeding of animals simply for slaughter is seen as wrong. Consider these questions:
a) Whatever your personal view on the rights and wrongs of the issue? Do you think that in 100 years' time Christians will be vegetarians?
b) How far is this debate really a debate about how to interpret the Bible?

3 Using Bible teaching and events as a basis for argument think of one reason in support of capital punishment (execution) and one reason against it.

4 Taking Bible teaching and the 'spirit' of the Bible into account, how would you use the Bible in approaching issues of sexual behaviour?

44 Is there any point in non-religious people reading the Bible?

The Bible was written by believers for believers, whether we are concerned with the Jews and their *Tanakh* or with Christians and their New Testament. That means that it makes certain assumptions about the readers, eg that they believe in God. Nowhere does the Bible try to prove God's existence, or even go off on an extended discussion about it. Its original readers would have viewed that as odd and unnecessary. What they wanted to know was what God was saying to them, or how he had spoken through Jesus. One of the writers of the hymns (psalms) very impatiently writes that it is only fools who 'say to themselves, "There is no god"' (Psalm 14:1). So much for them!

But although the Bible was written for believers, that does not make it a closed book to those outside.

As we have seen, for many people outside Christianity, or at least on the fringe, reading part of the Bible has sometimes been a quite decisive event in their lives. Hostage John McCarthy read the Bible because it was all he had to read in his captivity in Lebanon. He did not become a Christian, but he did feel that reading it gave him hope and vision. The Bible is not a magic book. All who read it will not be automatically converted to Christianity, nor should they expect to be. There is no claim to secret teaching, like in some of the books of the gnostics, a very varied collection of Christian fringe groups in the second century AD. Some of these claimed to have secret teaching passed on from Jesus or one of the disciples. The Bible is not that sort of book. There are no guarantees that reading the Bible will make readers Christian or Jewish or anything else. So non-religious people are not somehow locked out from reading the Bible. It will inform them about Christianity and its parent faith; it may alter some of the ideas they might have had about the Bible or Christian beginnings if they had been judging the Bible at second hand without reading any of it. But it will deceive no one. The Bible is also – humanly speaking – a supreme record of human experience and searching, of love, of loss, of joy and sorrow. No human reading it could fail to be touched by these themes.

It is important, however, in 66 so varied books to choose the most important books or bits of books. Non-religious people and religious people alike may have neither the time nor the patience to read the whole thing, nor do they need to. Not all bits are of equal value to everyone. Because of the age of the documents, it is helpful to read a commentary or introduction first so that puzzling or difficult bits can be explained. The whole aim is to make the Bible understandable to modern people. Some commentaries are mainly devotional, that is they are written for believers to help them in their religious or prayer life and they assume the reader is a believer. They might be intended for use with the person's daily Bible reading. Others are mainly academic, that is they do not assume that the reader has a personal faith and they aim to interpret the text in its time, sympathetically, but without taking the reader's Christianity for granted. These more academic commentaries may or may not be by Christians. It doesn't matter, when you look at their aim, whether the writers are Christian or not.

To investigate further

How many different reasons can you think of why people might read the Bible? To what extent do you think a person's motives for looking at the Bible are likely to determine what they get out of it?

45 Which bits of the Bible matter most?

For most Christians the final answer would probably be the Gospels. These provide the most detailed picture of Jesus as seen by four writers, each of whom presents the 'good news' - which is what the word gospel means - differently. Imagine a situation where part of the New Testament had to be lost. And at times in some countries where they have suffered the excesses of extreme political regimes, and new Bible distribution has largely had to rely on hand copying, such a thing could happen. In the last resort most Christians would want to hang on at least to the Gospels as the record of Jesus. Similarly, in translating the Bible into new languages, it is often the case that a Gospel is done first, to see how it goes and whether Christianity grows enough for the efforts and cost of additional translation and printing to be warranted.

Of course, not all Christians would always say that the Gospels were most important to them, and at different times in the history of

Christianity the value of different books seemed to stand out above the others. For instance, it seems that one of the aims of the book of Revelation is to encourage Christians who were under persecution, initially no doubt the persecution set in motion by the Roman emperor Domitian, who described himself as Lord and God. That was bound to lead to trouble with Christians and Jews, and the book of Revelation is seen by many interpreters as encouraging Christians through the hard times of suffering to look ahead to God's final triumph over all evil, and even death itself. So they might have chosen that, or 1 Peter as a favourite. It depends in the end on the individual and the circumstances in which they are living. Psalm 23, 1 Corinthians 13, and John 1 have proved popular with many Christians over the years.

That is one way of looking at the question. However, in considering which bits matter most many people would want to go back a stage. The area where the attitude of different groups towards parts of the Bible is most obvious concerns the bits between the testaments. Following the example of the Jews at the council of Jamnia, over a thousand years before, Protestant groups in their early days removed the Apocrypha/Deuterocanonicals from their Scriptures. Roman Catholic and Orthodox groups kept it; the latter viewing these books as having similar authority to other books in the Old Testament. In that sense the churches were advising their members about the importance, or lack of it, of one section of the Bible they received.

Today the authority of one set of books against another is unlikely to be an issue of live debate amongst the churches. Moreover, in practice there seems a fairly broad agreement over which books are of particular value for regular study of the Bible. Because the letters in the New Testament deal with practical issues of Christian behaviour (ethics) they are often studied carefully in church Bible study groups, where the members are involved in the very practical and ethical questions of everyday Christian living or in Religious Studies GCSE courses. But we should be careful not to forget books because they may not have received a lot of attention for a while. The Old Testament book of Amos has been 're-discovered' by many Christians who are finding relevance in his concern for justice and for national, international, commercial, and everyday behaviour that matches the religious beliefs people may claim. Some Christians would want to say that the 're-discovery' of particular bits of the Bible like this, at particular times in Christian history, is no accident, but the prompting of the Holy Spirit. So the question of which part of the Bible matters most has in the end no simple answer. It is a matter of personal choice, but to Christians it is also a matter of the message of God for their time and place.

We don't have to assume that each bit of the Bible is of equal value to everyone. A flick through the pages of the book of Leviticus will not reveal vast amounts of important material for city societies of today. This is because the book is mainly concerned with laws and detailed rules for the Hebrews, about sacrifices (chapters 1–7), skin diseases (13 and 14), even mildew (13:47–59; 14:33–57) – but within this book there is still important material for modern Jews about Yom Kippur and the Day of Atonement, including its origins and regulations – and underlying it is the belief that God wants humankind to live ethically. Ploughing through the Bible from cover to cover is not nearly as vital as studying the significant sections thoroughly, but at different times and in different societies people will turn to what seems relevant to them then. In time of war, particular passages may seem relevant; in time of famine, others; in times of comfortable prosperity, different passages will challenge people to leave their self-satisfaction behind; in times of dull church worship, particular passages will challenge the church to new life. This will be true in a Christian's personal life. If a close relative has died, particular passages may help; at a time of anxiety, others, and so on.

The same would be true of Jews answering which part of their Bible was most important. Most Jews might say the Torah, which forms the first five books of what to Christians is the Old Testament. For although the word law is sometimes used to describe the contents of the Torah, it includes stories and history and other material, all of enormous importance to Jews. It tells how they became a people and how God rescued them and gave them a land and an agreement or covenant by which to live. But for different individual Jews and at different times in the very troubled history of the Jewish people, different passages and different books will stand out.

46 How should the Bible be read for the first time?

It matters that we should read a book of the Bible from start to finish, unless it is a very long one, without interrupting it by looking at commentaries every few lines. Read an introduction in a commentary (some Bibles have them at the start of each book of the Bible). Then read the whole book so that it can be felt and taken in as a whole. Then go to the detail in the commentary on passages or points that are puzzling. Few adults have ever read a Gospel from cover to cover; they may have read bits, or heard bits read out in churches. Reading the whole book will remind you what it is, first and foremost: a book, written originally to stand separately from others. So a menu for reading the Bible could, look like this:

> # Starters
> The Gospel of Mark
>
> # Main courses
> 1 Corinthians
> The Gospel of John
>
> # Desserts
> Philemon
> Genesis 1–11

It is sometimes useful to discipline one's reading by writing beforehand, 'What I expected', afterwards, 'What I found' and, for more investigation, 'What puzzled me'. A sort of personal book review, which may help you to approach the books with fresh eyes.

To investigate further

Read one of the books from the menu above and try the suggested 'book review': 'What I expected', 'What I found' and 'What puzzled me'. If short of time, try reading Philemon. If you can't get a commentary the GNB introduction will do.

Thought-prompters

1 Why do you think few Christians have read a book of the Bible from beginning to end in one sitting? What do you think are the dangers of only reading a book in short sections?

2 Look at any commentary. Can you tell from the cover or the introduction whether it is mainly devotional (religious) or academic (assuming no religious belief on the reader's part)? What gave you the answer?

47 How do people find things in the Bible?

The simple answer to this question is through the system of references. Over the years thousands of editions of the Bible have been published. Some have been small enough to slip inside a jacket pocket. Others have been large enough to stand out clearly to people sitting fifteen rows back when placed at the front of a church. Now we have electronic copies to fit the pocket or handbag. Then there's the problem created by different languages. The Bible has been translated into hundreds of languages – some of which express an idea in a few words and some of which take several times more. It would therefore be quite impossible to supply page numbers to a passage for all Bibles. However, by giving three pieces of information any section can be found reasonably quickly in any Bible. The first item in the reference is the name of the book – Matthew, Mark, etc. The second is the chapter, and the third the verse. Thus, Mark 7:3 means Mark chapter 7 verse 3. In the Bible itself the chapter number is almost always printed in larger or darker type than the verse.

In the majority of Bibles that are published today the books are in the same order. The only exceptions to this usual order are some Bibles that include the Deuterocanonicals or books of the Apocrypha and place them between books of the Old Testament. Other Bibles put the Deuterocanonicals or Apocrypha in one section between the Old and New Testaments.

Many who use the Bible regularly, therefore, know roughly the position of each book and so quickly find the verse they are looking for. For those who are not so familiar with the order of the books, Bibles have a list of contents, so readers can look up the number of the page on which a book starts in that particular edition. Sometimes references give the books of the Bible as an abbreviation, eg Gen for Genesis, Ex for Exodus, and Mt for Matthew. Often a list of these abbreviations is given with or near the contents page.

So if you know the book, chapter, and verse, you can find any sentence in any Bible. However, knowing the reference is often the problem. You might vaguely remember the Bible says something about loving your neighbour as yourself, but you don't have much idea of where to start looking for it. This is where a concordance is useful. A concordance is a sort of Bible index. If you look up a keyword which features in the phrase you remember, say in this case 'neighbour', the concordance will give you references for all the occasions on which 'neighbour' is mentioned – along with six or seven words around it. So you will see amongst other references 'love your neighbour as you love yourself Mt 19:19'. A concordance also helps to trace a key Bible word, such as 'faith'. You can then look up the passages in which the word occurs and compare what they say. There are different concordances for different translations of the Bible. So you need a GNB concordance for a GNB Bible and an NIV concordance for an NIV Bible – otherwise the keywords may be different and you would not find all the references you needed.

Thought-prompters

Modern concordances are produced with the aid of computers. The concordance to the Good News Bible contains over 250,000 references and took four years to produce. One of the first concordances involved the work of 500 Dominican monks. Imagine listing every significant word in the Bible with its book, chapter, and verse, and then arranging them all in alphabetical order. One of the most famous, still in print, was compiled by Alexander Cruden. It became a life's work and at one time drove him to mental illness for which his friends had to commit him to a lunatic asylum. On one occasion he escaped and sued them, unsuccessfully, for putting him in!

Why do you think people went to the trouble to produce this aid to Bible study?

48 Is the Bible a children's book?

Lots of children are given Bibles, sometimes by relatives who don't always check that the text is in modern English or whether there are illustrations or what sort of illustrations there might be. Some children read and enjoy the Bible a lot, but others find it puzzling or boring. For children, and some adults, bits of it certainly are.

The books of the Bible were written by adults for adults with adult purposes in view. When the books were written, children were considered to be of minor importance. Their views didn't matter. In the Roman empire you could even have a troublesome child executed, and every year this seems to have happened to a dozen or so. Against this background Jesus surprised his contemporaries by taking children seriously (Mark 10:13–16) and by wanting to spend time with them. The Bible writers were concerned with getting their message across to adults, however, and wrote with them in view. So the Bible was not written as a book for children.

That does not mean that children cannot read it, or that it is totally unsuitable for them. Many great books were not written for children, but young people can read them, with proper help. There are adults who will testify that being made to study Shakespeare put them off; but there are many children who have enjoyed a good murder thriller like Macbeth with a bit of help to understand parts of it. The best help would be to make sure that the version or paraphrase young people use is readable, with good illustrations if possible, and to help them with the choice of passages. Perhaps adults should admit to children that the Bible has its fair share of murders, thrills, and spills, which might well make fiction books seem feeble by contrast. Of course, this is not to suggest that the significance of the Bible for children is as a source of murder narratives. Rather, dealing with humans at their deepest will naturally lead into narratives of good deeds and bad, love and hate, goodies and baddies (but with good and bad in everyone), forgiveness and revenge, death and resurrection.

What about younger children, such as the nursery–infant age range? In lots of creative ways, children can be introduced to biblical material. 'Godly Play' is one approach among many, including Scripture Union's *Bubbles* and *Tiddlywinks* programmes. Godly Play aims to tell biblical and other religious stories using three-dimensional materials, inviting listeners to enter the stories and connect them with their personal experience. The room in which the event occurs is vital and is carefully prepared – the children are involved in this, with perhaps a prayer corner, an area for Old Testament narrative images, another for the Gospels etc. It is seen as a place of peace in which the presence of God can be experienced. The story is told and never read. Collective and individual responses follow, including 'doing' and 'creating' where appropriate.

There is a 'wondering period', which includes questions like:

I wonder what you like best about this story?

I wonder which is the most important part?

I wonder where you are in this story?

I wonder if there is any part we could leave out, and still have all the story we need?

It is not only within Christian communities that biblical narrative is presented in ways like this; it is also used in holiday clubs, drama, crafts, musicals and multimedia presentations, and in formats like Bob Hartman's *Storyteller Bible*. The people involved are not sitting passively reading a book but are actively involved in a three-dimensional way – doing as well as being.

Thought-prompters

1 Some children's Bibles present the whole thing in comic-strip pictures, complete with thought bubbles and speech balloons. What do you think are the advantages and disadvantages of this?

2 'No one should be given a Bible until they are at least 13, and then it should be an adult version.' What do you think? Why do you think anyone should have such firm views as to say something like this? Do you think many adults would feel they had missed out on anything they could not catch up on if they hadn't discovered the Bible until the age of 13?

3 'The believing community should be centred on the Risen Christ. We encounter and learn about the Risen Christ in the believing community and in its scriptures, the Bible.'

But what if the community of believers has lost this vision?

4 Find about more about different approaches of working with the Bible with young children. If you are a member of a faith community, consider what approach might help your group in work with nursery and infant children.

49 What do young people think about the Bible?

The Biblos Project, sponsored by the UK Bible Society and carried out by the University of Exeter Religious Education team, set out to find out what young people know and think about the Bible and what has shaped their views of it. The first report, *Echo of Angels* (1998), argued strongly that biblical narratives should not be turned into secular stories or morals in the re-telling and that we should always remember that the 'hero' of the Bible, from a literary point of view, is God. Classroom texts on each of these themes have been produced for KS2 and KS3 children in RE by RMEP (Religious and Moral Education Press).

In the second phase of the research, reported in *Where Angels Fear to Tread* (2001), 700 secondary school children surveyed in Lancashire and Devon were unenthusiastic about the Bible as an authoritative text. This is hardly surprising in a society where immense emphasis is put on the 'freedom' and rights of the individual. They did not want to be told what to believe. However, they were prepared to engage with biblical narrative when they were allowed or encouraged to question, disagree or develop their own view.

In the third phase of the project, 1066, an easy number to remember, young people from school Years 6, 9 and 12 were asked about the Bible, and also about their religious beliefs (if any) and their hobbies and what mattered to them in life. This was reported in *On the Side of the Angels* (2004).

The profile of these young people in the 1066 sample corresponded closely to the 2001 National Census return on religion. For instance, 70.5 per cent described themselves as Christian, compared with National Census 71.6 per cent, and 15.1 per cent described themselves as having no religion (census 15.5 per cent). The research revealed some surprises. Perhaps the biggest was that young people were not hostile to the Bible as such. On the contrary they treated it with respect. Only 15.7 per cent thought the Bible was 'a waste of time'. As many as 65.4 per cent thought it is important because 'it tells us about God'; 52.2 per cent said the Bible is 'the Word of God'; 62.6 per cent said it teaches right from wrong; and 56 per cent said it can help when times are hard. In the light if this, the next two responses were perhaps surprising:

I respect the Bible and its teachings but do not live by it (63.1 per cent)
The Bible is important but I don't read it (63.1 per cent).

Perceptions of the Bible were directly related to the lifestyle of the young people. Young people whose hobbies were reading, voluntary work, youth groups or performing arts were more positive towards the Bible. Young people whose major hobbies were cinema, TV, PC games and sport were more negative towards it. Readers of fiction were more positive towards the Bible. Readers of PC magazines, car or motorbike magazines were more negative. Viewers of TV soaps or dramas were more positive; viewers of TV sport more negative. Girls were more positive then boys. As a sound bite we can say that those who are into 'human needs and long reads' (mainly the girls) are more positive towards the Bible while those who are into 'acts and facts' (mainly the boys) were less positive.

Currently the Biblos research team is working on the attitudes of New Zealand young people towards the Bible. The point of this is to examine whether in NZ and in other English-speaking countries that are culturally different from the UK, cultural factors are affecting how young people view the Bible. Might they be indoctrinated against it by factors in their culture? The whole question of indoctrination against religious belief in Western culture has been investigated further in my book, *Indoctrination, Education and God – the Struggle for the Mind* (SPCK, 2005). It would be a strange irony if our culture, which was produced in large part by the Bible, is now indoctrinating people against it. More information about the project and copies of these reports and can be obtained from biblos@exeter.ac.uk

Tricia Williams conducted research into the use of the Bible in the 11 to 14 age range within Christian communities. She found that the role of the believing community is crucial for young Christians' engagement with the Bible. She raised the question whether some adult Christians have lost their holistic sense of the Bible, with its Christ-centred narrative, as being central and authoritative in their faith. She found that study groups were seen by participants as a 'safe place' to engage with the Bible. Groups offered more stimulus, social as well as spiritual, than private study alone could offer. The best starting points into the text were found to be contemporary issues and current experiences of members of the group. Resources to assist group study, such as those provided by Scripture Union, were found to be important, but the willingness of members of the group to engage and the willingness of leaders to offer 'illustrative' leadership rather than dominate or seek to control the group's engagement, were equally important. One interviewee provided a view of what the Bible can be to a young Christian: 'it's like having an angel on your shoulder'.

Thought-prompters

1 Read the 1066 survey results again carefully. What – if anything – surprises you? Why? What do you think the implications of them might be for Christian groups who want to interest young people in the message of the Bible?

2 In the Biblos survey young people's comments were anonymous. Below are four of them, identified by their questionnaire number. How far do you agree with them? What are the implications of what these young people in Year 9 (age 13+) are saying for the churches?

I think the church needs to punk up a bit, when talking about the Bible (708).
It [the Bible] is not the kind of thing that can be judged as 'cool' or 'uncool' (974).
The Bible ... was designed to defeat the problem of anarchy, as it is a law presented to have eternal consequences (1034).
What's the point in it [the Bible] when you believe in God – why do you need proof if you believe? (1035).

3 Find a young person from a Christian community and ask them about their experiences of the Bible. Do they agree with the research?

50 How is the Bible used in schools?

In the UK, schools are divided broadly into two sorts, foundation schools – often of Christian foundation, but sometimes Jewish or Muslim or other religion – and 'community schools' (non-religious foundation). About one third of the nation's schools are church schools, mainly Church of England and Roman Catholic, but with a sprinkling of Methodist, Quaker, Seventh Day Adventist, non-denominational evangelical etc. Jewish schools naturally use the Hebrew Bible (Christian Old Testament) in their worship and in their religious teaching. Muslim schools use the Qur'an. In Christian and community schools the Bible may well be used from time to time in collective worship ('assemblies'), with a passage being read and perhaps commented on, in the hope that it may be of spiritual benefit to the hearers. In practice the selection of passages does not often happen in a coordinated way, so that well-worn narratives like the Good Samaritan keep re-appearing. The Biblos surveys suggested that this, along with the Prodigal Son, was remembered by pupils – although often they or their teachers had sometimes reduced them to secular morals (help people in need, forgive other people, or, in the case of David and Goliath, stand up to bullies, etc). As many as 76.5 per cent of those surveyed could name and accurately describe a passage from the Bible, – but 36.3 per cent went on to give a secular meaning or interpretation of their chosen passage.

In Religious Education syllabuses the Bible will usually appear in two ways. One may be within a unit on sacred writings, often in Year 7 or 8 (ages 11+ and 12+). Here the scriptures of several religions will be explored and an attempt made with young people to examine what it means to have a special book, the idea of revelation, the concept of Scripture itself as a rule or guide or signpost. It is an attempt to explain briefly what the Bible represents to Christian believers and what its significance is, rather than to go inside it and examine specific claims or particular narratives or questions of interpretation. Done well, it provides an overview of what the Bible is and means to Christians and also demonstrates the differences between the Bible and the sacred writings of some other religions.

In addition to this, specific biblical narratives will be studied at every level of RE (not always from the pages of the text itself) – from the Christmas narratives, perhaps in the infant reception class, to selected ethical sayings of Jesus in the GCSE short course in Year 11 (age 16+). The Education Reform Act (1988) required RE to reflect the fact that the religious traditions of the UK are in the main Christian, as well as teaching the principal world religions present in the UK. So in most school years children study Christianity and one other religion. Over 11 years of compulsory schooling they therefore encounter major teaching about Christianity. It is within this context that biblical narratives are used, to illustrate Christianity as a living religion rather than as ends in themselves. We can be proud that there are currently more pupils entered for GCSE Religious Studies in England and Wales than for History, Geography or French. (But RE still does not have enough specialist teachers).

Hebrew Bible/Christian Old Testament figures are still taught in primary and secondary schools, sometimes as part of of Jewish studies but more often in the context of Christian studies. Since some of these figures are also respected as prophets in Islam (eg Adam, Abraham, Moses, Joseph, David) they provide an opportunity to study the different ways in which these three monotheistic faiths view them. The life of Jesus is commonly taught in a one-term course in Year 8 (age 12+), often in 12 to 14 lessons of approximately one hour in length. Biblical options are offered in sixth form Advanced Level Religious Studies, although they are not nearly as popular as the Philosophy of Religion and Ethics options. Even in Ethics, biblical passages are used to illustrate Christian responses and debate about controversial moral and ethical situations. So the Bible is alive and well in good school Religious Education.

In other European countries, biblical narrative is used in similar ways in RE, though the curriculum varies from country to country. In the USA, where RE does not often occur in 'public schools' (which in the UK are known as 'state schools') biblical narrative is being taught in some high schools, either as a literature option or within comparative religion courses. So although sometimes people are heard to say that biblical teaching has disappeared from schools, this is not the case.

Thought-prompters

1 Except in independent (private, usually fee-paying) schools, RE has to be taught from an 'agreed syllabus'. The law requires the syllabus to be agreed between various interested parties, including the churches. Find out about the agreed syllabus for the area in which you live and where the Bible or biblical narrative appears in it.

2 Think back to your own days at school. Was the Bible used in RE? Well or badly? What are your main memories of it? If in your schooldays you had a link with a faith community such as a church, how was the Bible used with young people there?

51 What next for the Bible?

It is obvious that the Bible has a long and distinguished past. Its influence is all around us in art, music, language and literature, the legal system, and architecture. It is easily available in the free world, in hotel bedrooms, by hospital beds, in prisons, libraries, bookshops, newsagents, even supermarkets, and of course in every church. Not many people in the UK live more than a few miles at the most from where they could buy a Bible. The Bible is still highly regarded in many families as a significant present. But that is not very different from the status and availability of Shakespeare. The Bible has a massive part in the cultural heritage of the USA, Europe and the UK – but it is much more than that.

There is a continuing demand for translations, for copies and for new versions of the Bible throughout the world; so, although its influence in the West might appear to be declining, it is currently exploding in many parts of the world.

Some people will remain fascinated by the Bible as great literature or as ancient history. Others will be fascinated by the way in which it is a seminal text for Western culture, giving rise to art, music, dance, literature, laws etc. Different individuals, and different societies in different periods of history, have felt that different passages or incidents have 'spoken' to them. For Christians the Bible is more special than all that, as they believe that God speaks through its words and changes people and societies. In that sense the Bible is not just a book from the past, but a book for the future.

INDEX

Essential 100

Want to start reading the Bible? *Essential 100* is a great place to start! Grasp the 'big picture' of the Bible's story!

Hardback version:
▼ 1 84427 012 2

Paperback version:
▲ 1 84427 103 X

Essential 100 and all other products listed here are available from Scripture Union Mail Order (0845 07 06 006) or from your local Christian retailer.

Children's Guide to the Bible

**The Bible is like a country waiting to be explored –
here's a guide to help children go where they like!**

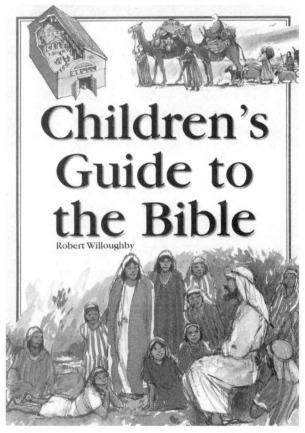

1 85999 072 X

Leading children through the Bible – from beginning to end –
Children's Guide to the Bible explains God's great plan for the
world.

Bible Alive!

Follow the routes of the great adventurers in the Bible and find out more about what really happened!

1 84427 069 6

A great book for children aged 8 and over. Can be used by individuals or in a group setting and is an ideal reference tool for looking at the geography and civilisations in the Bible.

Bible reading guides

Whatever your style, there's a guide to help you explore the Bible and discover what it's all about!

Encounter with God

Daily Bread

Closer to God

Snapshots
for 8 to 10s

One Up
for 11 to 14s